A faith to call our own

Quaker tradition in the light of contemporary movements of the Spirit

Alex Wildwood

Swarthmore Lecture 1999

Quaker Home Service

First published in 1999 by Quaker Home Service
Friends House, Euston Road, London NW1 2BJ

http://www.quaker.org.uk

© Alex Wildwood 1999

ISBN 0 85245 312 4

Design and layout: Jonathan Sargent
Text is set in 'Classical Garamond' from Bitstream
Printed by Norman Printing Ltd., Nottingham

Preface

The Swarthmore Lectureship was established by the Woodbrooke Extension Committee at a meeting held December 9, 1907: the minute of the Committee providing for an 'annual lecture on some subject relating to the message and work of the Society of Friends'. The name Swarthmore was chosen in memory of the home of Margaret Fox, which was always open to the earnest seeker after Truth, and from which loving words of sympathy and substantial material help were sent to fellow workers.

The lectureship has a twofold purpose: first, to interpret to the members of the Society of Friends their message and mission; and second, to bring before the public the spirit, the aims and fundamental principles of Friends. The lecturers alone are responsible for any opinions expressed.

The lectureship provides both for the publication of a book and for the delivery of a lecture, the latter usually at the time of assembly of Britain Yearly Meeting of the Society of Friends. A lecture related to the present book was delivered at Friends House, Euston Road, London, on the evening of May 1, 1999.

Dedication

To Seren, soul-mate and helpmeet,
who offers me the daily challenge to
love and be loved. Thank you for
believing when I doubted.

Acknowledgements

Many people have inspired, upheld and challenged me on my spiritual journey; here I acknowledge those who specifically supported or influenced me in this writing:

Harvey Gillman for eldering the Puritan in me and reminding me to walk *cheerfully* over the world; Janey O'Shea for her personal faithfulness and inspiring teaching ministry; Joyce Rawlings-Davies for loving spiritual friendship, laughter and transatlantic prayerful support (especially in the dark times); Ursula Windsor for tea and biscuits and many hours of honest dialogue; Ben Pink Dandelion, Marion McNaughton, Pam Lunn and Timothy Peat – for all the passionate, caring conversations and for being colleagues beyond the college; *all* the other Woodbrooke staff who have, in their different ways, helped to make that place my second home over the last four years; members of the Quaker Retreat Group (formerly QROOM) who have contributed so much to my experience and understanding of Quaker spirituality – in particular I appreciate conversations and worship with William West, Jeni Edwards, Anne Hosking, Ted Hoare, Brenda Wall and Linda Brasher; Rex Ambler for both his diligent scholarship and his generosity in offering his findings to others; Jane Horton for sharing her personal journey of descent, and for hospitality in London; Eric Maddern for hosting me while I wrote the 'zero draft' and for being the guardian of a wild and sacred place with many powerful associations for me; Jo Farrow and Val Ferguson for being firm but tender guides in the process of becoming a Swarthmore lecturer and author; Linda Batten, Ben Pink Dandelion, Elizabeth Wilkinson, William West and Kevin Redpath for helpful comments on the final draft; Tom Kelly for spiritual and writerly support; all the members of Nailsworth Meeting, who have (whether they knew it or not) released me to study and write during the last two years; Seren Wildwood for professional copy-editing in trying circumstances; and a final special 'thank you' to Lyn Longridge for the invaluable babysitting.

And I thank God for Hannah, born during the gestation of this lecture, whose joy and laughter help me to keep things in perspective.

Contents

Introduction 1

1 Awakening 7

2 My battered suitcase 12

3 Gifts of the Goddess 23

4 Body, self and soul 32

5 All my relations 40

6 Ritual and re-membering 47

7 Darkness and new life 59

8 Open to old light 71

9 Learning to pray anew 85

10 Stand still – and dance! 94

References 101

'After three hundred years we may be justified in taking an optimistic view of the achievements and resilience of the Quaker Way, and the success with which it has lived out its prophetic and conserving roles. However, to live the Quaker Way faithfully in our own time and land is not to try to repeat what early Friends were called to do, or to cling to whatever Quaker forms we have inherited in this Yearly Meeting. What we share with Friends who have gone before us is a task and some fine tools. Our task is to inaugurate the Way of God in this time and in this land; our tools are our personal experience of the Light Within, and our corporate experience in using collective guidance to discover and enact God's will in the world. To do this we must not become more like early Friends, but more like ourselves as we are in the eye of God.'
(Janey O'Shea, 1993 James Backhouse Lecture:13-14)

Introduction

In our meeting we recently considered the issue of the benches. Now ours is a historic meeting house, in continual use since the 1680s; the existing wooden benches, however, are not original but date from the eighteenth century and were only acquired by our meeting twenty years ago. The proposal was to replace with a circle of chairs.

Our subsequent discussions reminded me of a conversation between the Episcopalian preacher Matthew Fox and a young man he met in a Presbyterian church in Cardiff. Fox had just given a talk on 'Creation Spirituality and the Celtic Tradition' and was asked how the church, which usually attracted about 35 people to its worship, could be filled regularly, as it had been for his talk. He suggested removing the pews so that worship might become more physical, more spontaneous. 'Oh, we could never do that,' came the young man's reply, 'this parish is 150 years old.' Fox's reply is salutary:

> 'One hundred and fifty years is a tradition to be honoured,' I replied. 'But some day Christians are going to have to choose between their anthropocentric traditions and those of the universe, which is, after all, fourteen billion years old. Besides, if you remove the pews you might lose half of your congregation – say

about seventeen people – but you would gain hundreds more: artists, dancers, scientists, young people, and bored older people who are being excluded from worship by the headiness of it all.' (Fox, 1996:150)

I believe these words can 'speak to our condition' as British Friends at the end of the twentieth century. It is becoming a truism that we are unsure of our identity, have lost our former vigour, and are spiritually hungry (or, as it was better named in Meeting for Sufferings recently, we are suffering from *spiritual anorexia*, self-starvation).

Early Friends, it seems, rejoiced in a profound experience of escaping from religious dogma, of sharing a liberating sense of genuine enthusiasm (meaning 'God within'). They gladly accepted a discipline of surrender and obedience fired by a spirit of liberation, an infectious sense of hope and possibility. Whilst we can never return to a 'Golden Age', what is there in essence in Quakerism that is relevant for this 'postmodern' age? And perhaps as importantly, are we being led to radical departures from tradition in this time?

I was invited to write about my experience of contemporary 'stirrings of the Spirit', where I have encountered what we know as God both inside and outside the framework of traditional religious structures. Whilst our Advices and Queries invite us to be 'open to new light, from whatever source it may come' (*Quaker faith & practice*, 1.02.7), it is an all-too-human tendency to settle for the comfortable and the familiar. I certainly feel the conflict between the moderniser and the traditionalist within me. (I was for changing the benches but am considered a stickler for Quaker tradition in other regards.) Sometimes the tension between these different parts of myself seems creative, other times it feels merely schizophrenic. Our Quaker recognition of continuing revelation means we can never be complacent: as Friends we have chosen a spiritual path where we can expect to be disturbed and provoked. It's one of the things I love about us. But it also means, as Ben Pink Dandelion has pointed out, that we are a community in which, as we constantly move on, somebody is always grieving.

As I write of my spiritual 'openings' outside the mainstream Christian denominations I am describing a personal process of wrestling with the tradition. I have found that I cannot, as so many of my contemporaries do, simply walk away from the religious inheritance of my culture and consider it an irrelevance. At times this wrestling can feel very literal, even physical. Writing of his own Jewish community, Arthur Waskow describes them coming together around 'the effort, the hope – sometimes bright, sometimes flickering – to create a modern path of life that draws authentically from Jewish tradition but is expressed in new ways' (Waskow, 1978:2-3). Evoking the image of Jacob wrestling with the angel, he writes:

> We do not simply accept the tradition, but we do not reject it either. We wrestle it: fighting it and making love to it at the same time. We try to touch it with our lives. (Waskow, 1978:11)

In struggling to reconcile my Quaker identity with how I have experienced God in some unlikely places, an image has come to me of Friends today as 'a bridge people', a channel of mutual enrichment between those still within the Christian tradition and those searching outside it for a more life-affirming and personally meaningful spirituality.

In the eleven years since I joined the Society of Friends I feel I have been coming to terms with the distinctive Quaker experience of the Christian mystery, and in one way this present work is a 'progress report' on that journey. I have been haunted by the question posed to Damaris Parker-Rhodes when she and her husband were visited by Anna Bidder and William Thorpe during their application for membership of the Society. At the very start of the interview they were asked *what was the sense in which they felt they could call themselves*

Christian. For the four of them this was 'a primary question' (Parker-Rhodes, 1977:13).

Yet the deeper I have become involved with Friends the more that seems like the wrong question. Paradoxically, I have found that as 'the world' uses the term I do not want to identify as 'Christian' at all, and yet I have found myself led among Friends. I have felt drawn deeper and deeper into the heart of a mystery, but one clothed in cultural and historical garments which simply do not fit most of us any more. Sharing that process of questioning and discovery as honestly as I can is part of what I feel I have to offer.

One of the things which attracted me to Quakerism was the lack of hierarchical structures and religious leaders (as well as the absence of liturgies and creeds that had no meaning for me). I clearly recognise in myself an outstanding characteristic of present-day British Friends: *we will not be told what to do*. Whilst there is a healthy side to this anti-authoritarianism, there is also a great danger. There is mounting evidence that, lacking a common story, a shared religious vocabulary and understanding, we are having difficulty in reaching real unity in our meetings for worship for business and therefore in discerning and uniting with concerns and 'owning' our corporate work as a religious society. As someone 'exercised' about this growing crisis of identity and authority, I have to take responsibility for my part in it.

I now see part of my rejection of authority as less a sign of spiritual maturity and self-responsibility than a manifestation of my woundedness, a symptom of how I try to avoid anything that reminds me of what I was taught as a child as Christianity. As a Quaker passionately committed to truth, I know the challenge is to engage in risky dialogue with those Friends who most challenge my own self-definition – which in my case means those Friends for whom the Christian story is more than simply one religious myth among many (which is what it is for me).

Part of the vision I explore here is of the need for us to help one another heal from such past hurts so that we can be open to truth, to obedience to God, in the here and now. I believe we all carry 'baggage' from the past – unfinished business, congealed hurts and painful memories – that stop us being present in the moment, available to reality as it is and not as we imagine or would like it to be. I think it is part of the function of a healthy community of faith to help people deal with these limitations (which otherwise tend to solidify into prejudices and dogmas) and move on. I have heard some Friends say that their ministry has been inhibited or even 'eldered' by others for being too 'Christian' or for mentioning God. It is vital that we each feel free to speak *from experience* in the language that is meaningful to us; understanding then emerges in genuine dialogue, which I believe is deeply part of Friends' way. I hope we can all have the courage of our 'convincements'.

At one stage of my writing I was asked to summarise what I was saying to Friends. I wrote without hesitation:

- We are currently living through a time of tremendous cultural change, which necessarily includes a re-formulation of how we view ourselves and God. How we articulate and practise our Quaker faith will evolve in the light of this shift – which has been described as a second Renaissance.
- Whether we see it clearly yet or not, a new spirituality is emerging, one which reclaims much of what was lost in medieval Christianity. The sacred integrity of the body, of the earth, of the 'feminine' and of the experience of the Self is being recovered by groups both inside and outside the mainstream churches.
- Quaker spirituality, the discipline of inwardness and waiting, of turning to the Light – and thus transformed, working for 'the reign of God' on earth – has a potential today far beyond its cultural and historical Christian roots.

I do not directly address here our structures, our committees, our work of witness 'in the world'. I believe any problems we are having with these are rooted in the more fundamental issue of how our spiritual discipline, our understanding and vision of Quaker faith, must be articulated and modified for this 'new age of the Spirit'.

It has been a great challenge to write in a personal way as I was asked to do, for I was painfully aware that in the discipline of spiritual biography it is not the 'I' that is important but the struggles and surprises of the encounter with the Other. Yet I know that when any of us dares to write or speak 'from the heart' we touch a universal chord, we transcend the particular and tug the threads of our common humanity. Even so, a purely experiential account risks alienating those readers who cannot identify with the life path of the author. But experience is inevitably wedded to ideas, to an understanding of where we have been and where we think we are going. I hope Friends find a balance in these pages.

This is not a 'rags-to-riches' story of how I followed other spiritual paths and finally arrived at the 'true faith' of Quakerism. I have not rejected but rather *incorporated* earlier insights and experiences – and those have in turn been 'reframed' by my Quakerism. Unlike those biographies of Quaker 'saints' of earlier generations (which were wisely published posthumously and edited for sanctity) this personal journey cannot be read as a model for anyone else (God forbid!). I offer it merely as an encouragement to others to reflect on and risk telling their pilgrim's tale, as honestly as they can.

Nailsworth, January 1999

1   Awakening

With isolated exceptions, every generation prior to
ours has lived with the assumption that other
generations would follow. It has always been assumed,
as an integral part of human experience, that the work
of our hands and heads and hearts would live on
through those who came after us, walking on the same
earth beneath the same sky. Plagues, wars, and personal
death have always taken place within that wider
context, the assurance of continuity. Now we have lost
the certainty that we will have a future. I believe that
this loss, felt at some level of consciousness by
everyone, regardless of political orientation, is the
pivotal psychological reality of our time.
(Macy, 1991:5)

I first met Joanna Macy, a Buddhist scholar, social activist and
anti-nuclear campaigner, in the mid-1980s in one of her
workshops designed to help people share what they felt about
the possibility of nuclear war. She called this 'despair and
empowerment' work because in addressing what we felt – often
despair, anger, numbness or apathy – and daring to name the things
our culture wanted to deny, we experienced an empowering
sense of our connection to others, a transforming experience of

who we really are. As the work developed, participants began to share not just what they felt about 'the state of nuclear terror', in Joel Kovel's telling phrase (Kovel, 1983), but also their reactions to the loss of species, the destruction of habitats, the diminishment of our air and soil and water, their responses to the developing ecological crises of our age.

From this work I gained an extraordinary sense of the privilege and responsibility of being alive today. For whilst we are assured that human technical ingenuity will meet the planetary challenges we now face, more and more of us feel in our hearts that something is terribly wrong. We are realising that our present way of life is unsustainable and that 'more of the same' is not going to save us. We sense intuitively that something more radical, more visionary, is called for.

For this is a time of transition on a truly global scale, a time when the future is wide open, if fundamentally uncertain. It is a crucial time not only for humanity but also for the evolution of life on earth. As human activities bring about the extinction of an estimated 30,000 species every year (or three unique forms of life lost every hour) we are severing the evolutionary potential of whole branches of the tree of life. And as we begin to 'modify' the genetic structure of plants and animals we are disrupting the balance of life on earth as it has evolved slowly over millions of years.

This sense of threat and uncertainty, of living in a time of both danger and opportunity, is for me both the context in which we have to speak about faith but also a pointer towards an emerging new spirituality. For what I experienced in these workshops with Joanna and her co-leaders was how the political, economic and ecological crises we face reveal an underlying spiritual *malaise*; they are symptoms of our radical dissociation from one another, from the rest of life on earth, and from the compassionate core of our own being. When we were given permission to really experience what we felt about the state of our world and were then asked *why* we should care about the drowning of dolphins in tuna nets, the starvation of children in Eritrea, or the destruction of a local meadow which someone had known from their childhood, we were awakened to something much more profound than a merely conceptual *understanding* of the threats we face. What was offered to us was an immediate experience of compassion, the chance to feel how each of us is more than what Alan Watts called 'the skin-encapsulated ego' (Macy, 1991:183).

This experience of the interdependence of all beings is an awareness which now underlies all my understanding, as well as being central to my religious faith. 'Despair and empowerment' work combined spirituality, therapy and social action in one seamless whole. When Joanna took the work to what was then East Germany, Rudolf Bahro described it as 'true politics'. It broke through our collective denial, overcoming what psychologist Jay Lifton has named our 'psychic numbing' in the face of overwhelming threats to our survival. It restored hope, not in a superficial way but by consciously embracing our 'demons', our collective shadow. It was a pioneering synthesis which engaged heart and mind, body and spirit and which made no distinction between our personal pain (the brokenness of our individual lives and relationships) and the suffering of our world. In both cases healing came with bearing witness, with having our reality named.

Paradoxically, when we are literally bombarded by information on a daily basis, it is hard to keep 'the big picture' of our situation in conscious awareness. Faced with what I know at the deepest level of my being, I so easily feel overwhelmed, and seek to lose myself in compulsive activity, in 'busyness as usual'. To be present to what is before us, to remain aware of both the dreadful suffering and the miraculous beauty of our world (to 'sustain the gaze', as Joanna put it) requires great courage. It is actually a rigorous *religious* discipline, one which needs constant practice, for the tendency is to 'fall asleep' again, to close down to what we feel, to let numbness and despair or a sense of personal powerlessness overtake us once more.

At Yearly Meeting in 1988 we were encouraged to 'hear within us the sound of the earth crying'. These poetic words of Zen monk Thich Nhat Hanh are a literal and practical instruction in how to experience the spiritual truth of what he calls our 'interbeing'. As Joanna Macy used to say in these workshops: 'the heart that breaks is the heart that can contain the world'.

Along with the wholesale destruction of habitats and species, we are also in danger of losing what Susan Griffin calls 'a certain orientation, a map of the world, stories of creation, histories, and, along with all this, ways in which the world made sense and heaven and earth were connected in one pattern of meaning'. She speaks of 'a kind of disintegration, a fragmentation as an older order which once unified and explained experience fails' (Griffin, 1995:7).

In this extraordinary time I find myself both longing for, and totally unable to believe any more in, a super-parent God, an eternal omniscient Being who can intervene in human history to rescue us. It's not that I don't have experience of what I would call God – but that after Darwin, after Marx and Freud, after Einstein and quantum science and after the Holocaust and other twentieth-century horrors, I identify as what John Selby Spong, the bishop of Newark, New Jersey, calls 'a believer in exile', one of those for whom the theistic God of tradition, the omnipotent Sky-God, has finally lost all credibility (Spong, 1998:21).

If this is a common experience, what we are facing is a collective 'coming of age' which requires a new understanding of the divine and a new sense of spirituality which does not contradict what we know intellectually, emotionally or from personal experience as 'citizens of this century'. And that means challenging much of what organised religion has taught us; it also may mean personal healing from religious abuse and spiritual violation (see Linn *et al.*, 1995). At this crossroads point in human history, what is needed is a new religious sensibility, a different consciousness of who we are:

We human beings are not caught on the earth, alone, alienated, waiting for a more perfect world, a more perfect life, union with a distant God. We are at home here. We are at home as creatures who are born and die, creatures who love and fear. Our pain is here. Our ecstasy is here. (M. Susan Milnor, sermon quoted in Kasl, 1992:382)

As many of us struggle with a painful sense of exile from our tradition, and of bereavement and the loss of certainty known to previous generations, as we face the reality of the destruction of our world, the spiritual resources we have at our disposal can seem very meagre.

Sometimes at night, when I am tired of being forever a traveller, I look in through lighted windows and am nostalgic for the settled life. For a moment I long for a Bible, a Jesus, a guru, an authoritative word from beyond to guide me. But I know the price is greater than I want to pay. It seems less than gracious to abandon the authority I have been given for my life, frail and brief as it is. In this ordered and creative chaos that I will always be fashioning into the narrative of my life, I am sustained by an abiding trust that, as Isak Dinesen said, 'God made man because He loved stories'. Without my autobiography and yours, the story of the universe would be forever incomplete. (Keen, 1994:44)

Sharing our stories can seem such a paltry thing to do; yet our own experience as Friends of the value of personal journals and testimonies reminds us that stories are, in an important sense, all we have. It is all the more vital, therefore, for us to be aware of what we carry in our personal and cultural 'suitcase' – to articulate those formative experiences and sometimes painful histories which we all carry around and which influence who we are.

2   My battered suitcase

To find God we must let go of God. Then God will find us
with new breakthroughs of grace and divine experience.
The death-of-God issue that played so prominently in
our theologies of the late sixties was less the death of
divinity than a death of our old images of divinity. Now
we must begin to re-imagine from experience, learning
to trust our experiences of awe, wonder, darkness,
nothingness, creativity, compassion, justice, celebration
... A time like ours – a transition time – is a time for old
images of God to be buried and new ones to emerge.
(Fox, 1996:272)

I first attended Quaker meeting for worship just over twelve
years ago. I don't know quite what I expected that morning as
I walked past the entrance to Shrewsbury Meeting House and
then plucked up the courage to turn round and actually enter
the building. There, in the silence of my first meeting, I didn't
experience the often-reported sense of 'coming home' but
something else equally profound. For I found myself silently
weeping at the sight of a bible lying innocently on the table in
the middle of the room. It may sound strange but I felt a deep
sense of healing to know that it was just a book lying on a table
and not a weapon that would be used against me.

This may seem an extreme reaction; it certainly surprised

me. I had not grown up in a particularly religious family nor had I ever belonged to some extreme sect. My father was an American with Lithuanian Orthodox roots, himself an agnostic throughout his adult years. I received little in the way of overt religious education from him, but he did instill in me a love of nature and the outdoors. My mother was English, of Scottish Presbyterian descent, confirmed into that church as an adult, and when she became a church-goer I dutifully tagged along to keep her company. I only once remember us attending church together as a family – at Christmas, whilst on holiday in Switzerland. My parents neither read nor referred to the Bible, though as a young child I was enrolled with the Crusaders, where we were rewarded with sweets for each Bible passage learnt, so bribery, militarism and text were combined at an early age for me. Apart from this, my religious upbringing was confined almost entirely to the schools which I attended.

I went to a preparatory school which was founded by Quakers, because my mother believed it had a good academic reputation. Quakerism was not a prominent feature of the place. Although I had a brother four years older than me, when I think of my childhood, the word that comes to mind is 'solitary'. But if I did not easily form relationships with people, my solace came from hours spent in nature. Whilst other children create imaginary friends, I found the world of plants and creatures provided all the company I needed. At school and at home I pursued my fascination with natural history, reading avidly, creating my own museum of curiosities found in my travels and generally spending many self-absorbed hours exploring the stream at the bottom of the garden or venturing into the forbidden spinney beyond. My brother rarely shared in these adventures; he was always the gregarious, outward-going one, whilst I was content with the rich inner world of my own, happy to contemplate the mysteries of puddles, hedgerows and copses.

At this tender age I was fascinated by biology and human anatomy but masked my enthusiasm for the latter because I had already learnt that there was something not quite 'proper' about bodies and anything associated with them. I remember on a school Open Day being asked by a visiting parent what I wanted to do when I grew up. Without hesitation or irony I replied that I was going to be a missionary doctor. With hindsight I can see that I was one of those 'helpful' children who learn to take care of those around them, who want to be healers in order to mend their parents' unhappy marriage.

Later I was sent to boarding school, with its compulsory chapel attendance and daily prayers and soon all thoughts of missionary service left me. I came to hate the words, the meaningless, dreary forms, the doom and fearfulness of the 'Christian' religion instilled in us in its gloomy Victorian chapel. I actually started getting physically ill on Sunday evenings and was prescribed suitable medication to drug my recalcitrant colon into reluctant conformity. What I was learning as Christianity was inextricably tied up with the ideology of a British public school, where I was being groomed to be, if no longer a colonial master, then at least a captain of industry.

As I was made to sit in services and listen to words which had no meaning for me, which had no resonance with my own experience, I knew deep within me (though I had no words for this then) that my spiritual integrity was being violated. Over thirty years later, while I was a student at Woodbrooke, what I had experienced then was finally named for me. Referring to missionary activity amongst Australian aborigines, Janey O'Shea, the Quaker Studies tutor, prayed for forgiveness for the violence of 'the Christ imposed'. I don't think it fanciful to say that I know something of how the aborigines felt: the wild spirit in me was also forced into submission to an alien 'religious' ideology. At the time I rebelled silently, in my body, having no language to counter my indoctrination.

When, in the autumn of 1997, I attended a course at Woodbrooke on 'Quakers and Christ', Timothy Peat, the Bible Studies tutor – as part of what he called 'detoxification' – invited us to symbolise and write down our spontaneous associations with the words 'Bible', 'God' and 'Christ'. My drawing included a gruesome blood-dripping figure on a cross, marching soldiers with flags, a vast bible dwarfing a bewildered little stick figure, and regimented rows of a chapel congregation. The words that came to me were: pain, fear, superstition, sin, damnation, guilt and compulsory attendance. That was the Christian influence of my schooldays as I internalised it. Once I left school I not unsurprisingly rejected religion altogether.

Yet there I was many years later attending Quaker meeting – and I could not explain why. I just knew that something (I would not have been comfortable then to call it God) was definitely *leading* me. I remember one morning coming out of Shrewsbury public library, where I had been browsing the religious books, and having to sit down beside the front steps as I was suddenly moved to tears. But by what? I had no language for it then. Although at the time I was immersed in the world of psychotherapy, I knew that what I was feeling was not a personal grief. The tears were not even expressing sorrow as such; they were as much tears of joy, tears of acceptance and relief, tears of passionate caring. I certainly felt uncomfortable – this was not 'normal' and I was clearly not in control of myself. But I also trusted my inner sense that whatever I was being touched by *really mattered*. Whatever 'it' was that was reaching me in this unconscious way, I knew that acknowledging it, accepting it as a primary influence in my life, would be one of the most important decisions I would ever make.

If, like the majority of my generation, I had vehemently rejected established forms of religion, I still secretly yearned for a spiritual home, a place where I could again feel myself part of a Greater Mystery without compromising what I knew both intellectually and emotionally. Here, amongst Friends, was a point of access to the tradition of my upbringing where I would not be asked to subscribe to beliefs which I found literally incredible. Here was a group of ... Christians? – I wasn't sure if they were or not – with a place of worship lacking all the usual regalia, all the trappings of a church. This 'congregation' seemed to quietly accept all comers to their worship without imposing anything on them. They also had no visible hierarchy of figures of spiritual authority. All of which was very appealing to me in that first vital contact. Indeed, Quaker openness and trust in the freedom and equality of the call to vocal ministry has never ceased to amaze me. After only a few months of attending meeting it felt clear to me that I was meant to join Friends as my community of faith. At the time I could still hardly articulate what I meant by faith (or community for that matter).

About two days before my application for membership was to be considered by Worcestershire and Shropshire Monthly Meeting, I suddenly panicked. Visiting the elder whose kindly fielding of my questions had eased my passage towards membership, I shared with him my doubts, my sudden overwhelming alarm that I wasn't a 'Christian' and shouldn't be asking to join this body. Surely this couldn't be a true leading of the Spirit? He reassured me that it didn't matter. I think he said, 'That's not important' – whether he meant that I would grow in faith or whether he meant it was possible to be a Quaker and not be a Christian I don't know. Maybe he saw that my path would be to wrestle with this very dilemma for years to come!

Like many newcomers, I read avidly about Quakers, especially about the founding of the movement at the time of the English Civil War, when people felt 'the world turned upside down'. And I was captivated by how early Friends described being overwhelmed by a mystical experience that was profoundly rooted in the real world, in political reality and in the revolutionary upheavals of that time. Even though I 'screened out' much of the language which had unpleasant 'Christian' overtones for me, something in the experiences they described reached out beyond my twentieth-century scepticism and began to take hold of me. The early Quaker writings – as much as the experience of meeting for worship – touched my heart:

The Lord of Heaven and Earth we found to be near at hand; and as we waited upon him in pure Silence, our Minds out of all things, his Dreadful Power, and Glorious Majesty, and Heavenly Presence appear'd in our Assemblies, when there was no Language, Tongue nor Speech from any Creature, and the Kingdom of Heaven did gather us, and catch us all, as in a Net; and his Heavenly Power at one time drew many Hundreds to Land. (Howgill, 1672)

I was strongly drawn to the Quaker sense of religion as a way of life rather than a system of theology. I found the Quaker emphasis on the centrality of inward authority profoundly empowering. I came to understand Quakers as 'inside-out Christians' who conduct their worship and business 'without claiming religious insights which are untested by personal experience' (Heathfield, 1994:15).

But even as an opinionated newcomer I had an uncomfortable sense that there was something missing in the meetings I was attending, something it was now as much my responsibility as anyone else's to redress. Early Friends spoke much of the *power* of God at work in their meetings and I found myself wondering why I didn't often sense this among twentieth-century British Friends. What I did discover was a welcoming and friendliness, certainly, an acceptance of people as they are, an extraordinary tolerance that could embrace extreme diversity of belief, together with an active commitment to good causes of all kinds. But at the time I couldn't help feeling that all these fine traits were a pale shadow of what had previously illuminated Friends' lives. *Something* had burned within the souls of the founders of Quakerism; something more than political radicalism or ethical principles had *led them* in every aspect of their lives – one consequence of which was the social witness for which Quakers were renowned.

I was intrigued by the audacious, radical nature of the Quaker business method but also saddened by what I saw as the often deadening imbalance of administration over inspiration and by how, increasingly, other secular models – of democracy, consensus or business management – were creeping into this distinctive Quaker practice. Like many Friends I was drawn towards the spiritual alivencss at the fringes of the yearly meeting, the listed 'special interest groups' that have arisen in the past twenty years or so. In general, I got the impression of our yearly meeting as rather old and tired, as if we were living off the former glory and spiritual 'capital' of our ancestors.

I accepted that there could be no return to the seventeenth century, but still I sought the vivid experience of personal transformation early Friends described. What was William Penn referring to when he spoke of early Friends as being 'changed men themselves before they went about to change others. Their hearts were rent as well as their garments, and they knew the power and work of God upon them'? Did I detect in my contemporaries, as he did, that this power was manifest in 'the great alteration it made, and their stricter course of life, and more godly conversation (Penn, 1765:xviii)? Whether that was so or not, having been so put off by the meaningless liturgies and forms of school religion, I warmed to Penn's description of the mission of early Friends: 'The bent and stress of their ministry was conversion to God, regeneration and holiness, not schemes of doctrines and verbal creeds and new forms of worship, but a leaving off in religion the superfluous and the ceremonious and formal part' (Penn, 1765:xviii).

What these early Quakers seemed to be describing was an extraordinary breaking-in, a divinely-inspired disruption of their lives which empowered them to challenge all contemporary forms of outward authority, the temporal powers of church and state. Here was a movement that spanned all walks of life, that in a few short years took the country by storm, and provoked the government of the day to impose draconian powers to curtail it, whose followers were ruthlessly persecuted yet none of whom ever renounced their faith – even under pain of death or faced with the confiscation of all they possessed. Their courage and faith both inspired and amazed me, for the meetings I attended seemed related to this phenomenon in name only. As a zealous newcomer I wanted to know what had changed over the centuries and why!

Whenever I was part of a meeting that did not feel to me to be infused with the sense of 'being in the Life' that early Friends spoke of, I recalled Anne Wilson's stirring accusation to the young Samuel Bownas: 'A traditional Quaker; thou comest to meeting as thou went from it (the last time), and goes from it as thou came to it, but art no better for thy coming, what wilt thou do in the end?'(Bownas, 1795:3). Just as Bownas found this 'pat to my then condition', it seemed to be so to ours as well.

For the Quakerism I was encountering seemed to balance in equal measures radical potential with conservative contentment. Here and there were sparks of Life, but my overall impression was of a forgotten fire. Like many people coming to Friends in Britain since the Second World War, I know I selected the bits of Quakerism I liked and tended to ignore the rest. No wonder, perhaps, that like many others I found my spiritual needs were met more authentically elsewhere. Yet as I slowly opened myself to Friends' ways, I too began to feel the truth of Robert Barclay's experience of coming into 'the silent assemblies of God's people' and as I sensed 'a secret power among them, which touched my heart', I felt 'the evil weakening in me and the good raised up' (*QFP*, 19.21).

I came to Friends as 'a child of the sixties', a product of that extraordinary exuberant decade which, as Doug Gwyn notes, has certain parallels with Britain in the 1640s. In the mid-seventeenth century young people were 'shaken out of their inherited religion by the English Civil War ... the English national church lost credibility for them as a religious institution ... Where was the spiritual authority they could trust? ... England had become a battlefield of competing creeds, clergies and sacramental practices' (Gwyn, 1997). This was the seedbed of the Quaker movement. For my own 'Baby Boom' generation, coming of age in the 1960s, ours was a time of tremendous hope and optimism, of economic prosperity and cultural adventurousness. But it was also the time of the Vietnam war, and the possibility of political revolution hung in the air. Events in Paris and on campuses in the United States revealed how the universities were enmeshed with the vested interests of the 'military-industrial complex'. Going to college in Ulster in 1969, I was rapidly politicised by the sight of armed troops on British streets. Political radicalism combined with intellectual excitement and the questioning of values of all kinds. Studying sociology and anthropology, I was educated to the way societies define what is normative and police what is permitted. The lengths Western nations were prepared to go to in order to preserve our privileges and control of world markets were literally brought home to us during what has aptly been called 'the first televised war in history'.

Later, doing postgraduate research at Sussex, I learnt how developments in science were calling into question the very notion of a discrete and definable reality which by observation we can come to know in a dispassionate, objective way. Physics was probing the unpredictability of matter at the most basic, atomic level. It was moving away from a traditional model of a mechanical universe composed of separate bodies interacting like billiard balls into quantum theory's understanding that there is no objective reality 'out there' separate from our perception of it. The 'new physics' suggested we inhabit a *participatory* universe, where the act of observation subtly changes what we study.

Meanwhile, from anthropology I learnt that Western science is just one way of knowing. Researching the history of science, I discovered that scientific knowledge accumulates through successive 'paradigm shifts' and that what we think of as factual certainty about the universe is just a current working definition of reality. Instead of objective truth revealed by observation and experimentation, even science deals with probabilities. All this against a backdrop of cultural interest in shamanism and 'altered states of consciousness'. This was a decade of experimentation, of 'sex, drugs and rock 'n' roll'.

It was also the time of the founding of Greenpeace and their first dramatic anti-nuclear actions as well as their much publicised 'Save the Whales' campaign. Rachel Carson's *Silent Spring* dramatically heralded a whole new literature on ecological catastrophe. The mounting evidence of our deteriorating environment and the continuing possibility of nuclear war meant that the myth of unlimited growth and 'inevitable' progress was increasingly called into question. The awareness of 'limits to growth' meant that as young adults we felt both a deep sense of loss and an acute sense of responsibility – not just for our own lives but for the future of life on earth. It was a profound initiation.

From these college years I learnt that knowledge itself is socially constructed, that human language and concepts actually shape our perceptions of the social and material world around us, so that in an important sense our ideas and beliefs determine the very reality we take for granted as obvious or 'natural'. The awareness that there is always more than one way to define reality and the self-reflexivity that became a hallmark of art in the period were later to be labelled 'postmodernism', a self-conscious cultural style in which all knowledge could be seen as relative and objective truth replaced by competing 'narratives'. As a student I learnt to see human beings as actors in a script which we are improvising as we go along.

Throughout my student years I studiously avoided anything to do with 'religion'. Political ferment was my faith and Marxism its creed. I accepted Marx's definition of religion as the opium of the masses, a palliative that made people's lives seem bearable in the face of drudgery and oppression. The Christian groups on campus were objects of scorn and derision. I was a militant atheist, dismissing all talk of God as arrant nonsense and superstition. I believed in 'people power' and class war. Progress was human progress; the radicalism of the human spirit was what would change the world.

Yet during my three years of undergraduate study and in the nine months after my first degree, I spent countless hours beachcombing on the wild north Antrim coast. Walking along the strand in all weathers, enjoying the solitude for hours without meeting another soul, I would later identify strongly with those Celtic hermits of old who felt the presence of God in such windswept places, who heard in the cry of the gulls and felt in the lashing saltspray the untamed Otherness, the unspeakable and uncompromising nature of God. At the time I had no sense of a divine presence, I only knew I felt most content, most fully myself, alone on those windswept beaches.

The 1960s were a time of great questioning and cultural upheaval; it felt like an apocalyptic moment, an end time with the potential for radical new beginnings. Against the background of 'flower-power' hippie culture and talk of revolution 'by any means necessary', I married for the first time. Looking back I can see I was not conscious of the commitment I was making; it simply seemed the next logical step in what was clearly a significant relationship. We married in a registry office in London, making no reference to things Eternal.

3   Gifts of the Goddess

In the beginning was God
In the beginning
the source of all that is
In the beginning
    God yearning
    God moaning
    God labouring
    God giving birth
    God rejoicing

And God loved what she had made
And God said
    'It is good'
And God, knowing that all that is good is shared
held the earth tenderly in her arms
God yearned for relationship
God longed to share the good earth
And humanity was born in the yearning of God
We were born to share the earth

Excerpt from *Blessing the bread: a litany* (Heyward, 1984:49)

If in the 1960s I rejected the Christianity of my childhood and
defiantly proclaimed myself an atheist, in the 1970s I opened

once more to a sense of divine presence, but in a radically different context to that of the religion of my childhood. My first wife was in a women's consciousness-raising group and found employment in the emerging field of feminist publishing. I became involved in running 'Men Against Sexism' crèches and joined one of the few men's groups in London.

I began to meet women who spoke of the Goddess, the divine feminine, and who celebrated their religion in circles of personal sharing and in marking the cycles of nature and the seasons of the earth. Many of these groups were influenced by Starhawk, an American self-styled 'witch', who had published a highly influential book, *The Spiral Dance*, much used by such groups. These circles usually aligned themselves to some degree with Wiccan and other pagan revivals in this country. Approaching them with an open mind, I discovered nothing to confirm the prejudices of the mainstream culture.

Here were women (and a few men) reclaiming their power through imagery and symbolism that had meaning to them, creating rituals that reflected their own life experience. For many such groups there was a direct link between spirituality and political action. As in other areas of the Women's Movement at the time, the prevailing ethos was that 'the personal is political' and in this case the spiritual was political too. Finding myself often either the only man present or one of a tiny minority was salutary in itself. I didn't encounter much anti-male feeling as such, though the celebratory mood was encapsulated by the slogan of that time: 'the future is female'. What I did find in the mixing of the spiritual and the political was a sobering recognition of how sexism affects women, children and the planet and how gender polarities distort all our lives. I found there a realisation of what male violence was about: a fundamental, historical separation from nature – both the nature of the earth and the nature within us, our feelings, intuitions and imaginal life.

These circles were different from anything I had encountered in the religious culture of my childhood. For one thing we often met outdoors. We were constantly reminded of the elements of creation all around us, the physical world of which we are a part. Nature was not worshipped as such, as paganism's detractors imagine. Rather, there was a sense of the year as a wheel turning, with festivals celebrated according to observable changes in the phases of the moon, the length of day and night, or the harvests of the earth. These rites resonated with this land and with our senses; they brought home to me that 'pagan' and 'heathen' both simply mean 'country-dweller' – and were made derogatory terms (as 'Quaker' also was) for political purposes. These terms simply refer to the pre-Christian folk-wisdom of these and other lands, the aboriginal and popular forms of religion and native lore that the medieval Church fought long and hard to suppress.

It is no incidental prejudice that the things which patriarchal masculinity and its representatives in the Church most reviled were things they were most afraid of – particularly the association of women's bodies and sexualities with the wild, 'capricious' forces and rhythms of nature. In these circles I discovered a profound respect for the divine gift of physical reality. Our bodies were not considered separate from the body of the earth, nor any less sacred. There were leaders of these rituals but their roles arose from their sharing of their knowledge and skills. The rituals were created by all those present; everyone was involved in an active way, with a general encouragement of creative expression.

I learnt here that worship could involve the whole of one's being; that liturgy (which means 'the people performing') need not be imposed but could arise from the participants' own experience; that forms of worship come alive when they invite spontaneous creative expression; that our imagination and feelings are a literally vital part of effective worship. Here the acknowledgement of personal struggles and choices, as well as the celebration in community of people's achievements, were central aspects of worship itself. Nothing was too commonplace or mundane ('of the earth') to be thought unworthy of our celebration and thanksgiving.

I don't wish to portray this movement as an Arcadian idyll; it certainly wasn't, and we embodied many contradictions (such as driving cars to remote places to honour nature there). But it was a vital step for me in reclaiming a sense of religion as a 'binding back' (re-ligere), an experiential acknowledgement of our dependence on the earth and its seasons, its productivity and cycles. It was a powerful antidote to the alienation of our industrial civilisation and mainstream religion.

It was in the context of these pagan circles that I had a profound experience that forever changed my sense of faith. I was part of a group of men and women who had gathered to celebrate the Summer Solstice (the longest day of the year) at Laurieston Hall in south-west Scotland. One morning I went with a friend to visit a nearby neolithic site known as Cairn Holy. This consists of two burial mounds whose chambers have collapsed, leaving only the largest stones of the original structures exposed. We parked the car and walked to the first mound, feeling the power and peacefulness of this place where people had gathered for religious ceremonies so many centuries before. It was a particularly beautiful site, near the head of a small valley that stretched down to the sea.

We made our way to the second, smaller grave, which was in a more exposed situation than the first, less welcoming, yet powerful in a different way. As we began to walk back to the car, deep in thoughtful conversation, we passed the first group of stones again. I suddenly 'knew' I had to go and lie face down on a huge recumbent stone that lay beside the entrance to the tumulus. As I lay down on this rock, which was both deeply cold and yet superficially warmed by the summer sun, I momentarily lost my usual sense of who 'I' am. My identity as a separate being dissolved, I *became* the stone I was lying on, as well as the grass and sorrel growing in the foreground, the fields in the distance and the sea beyond. There was no distinction between 'me' and any of these other elements of existence.

It was not a frightening experience, yet after it nothing would ever seem the same again. I experienced the world as a different place, though everything looked as it had before. I remember it as a breaking-through, a glimpse of a way of knowing reality that I cannot live day by day but the awareness of which changes everything. I knew it was not something easily spoken about, yet nor was it something I would ever wish to deny. Even now it feels strange to name it. But it is something I have known 'experimentally' and I know now that such experiences are far more common than was once acknowledged. (See, for example, Dorothea Abbott's article 'The Oceanic Experience' in *The Friend*, 17 July 1998.)

Looking back, it seems no coincidence that this return to a sense of the spiritual reality underlying our lives should have occurred in the company of women. The (Native American) Lakota peoples have a saying, 'All things are born of woman'. Whilst I do not suppose divinity is literally engendered, if I want to imagine it that way, it makes far more sense to me to visualise it as female, as a birthing and nurturing Power sustaining the whole of creation. This sense of female primacy (which is, after all, reflected in our biology: as human embryos we all begin as female) is contained in the word *matrix*, the linguistic family of matter and material, the 'maternal' ground of all being.

This kind of inclusive imagery has become for me far more than a matter of 'political correctness'; it is a vital witness to the complexity, the inclusiveness and mystery of what we are called to worship. The language and imagery of women has introduced me to a different understanding of both divinity and faith:

> All my life, I've heard 'God is love', without understanding what was meant. Recently I've come to feel that in a very real way G-d/ess IS the love that flows in and between and among us. The ebb and flow of my commitment to love, to peace, to harmony makes G-d/ess stronger or weaker in my heart.
>
> Sometimes the web feels like G-d/ess' body, her vast cosmos, of which we are an inextricable part. The web is

also the love that flows through creation, from G-d/ess,
from us, from everywhere. The web is an affirmation
and comfort, support and clear-naming. The web is
harmony, proving to me by its fleeting, fragile
appearances that peace can happen. Most of all, for
me, the web is friendship.

That the web exists is my faith. Spinning at it,
dancing along with it, and calling others into it are my
ministry. Ripping it or withdrawing into isolation and
despair are my sins. (Ketterer, 1987:11)

Rose Ketterer explains her use of the name 'G-d/ess' as an
attempt to convey the difficulty of naming the divine, and is
honest enough to admit that 'the usage is mostly consciousness-
raising with a bit of Quaker obstinacy about honesty in
language' (Ketterer, 1987:11). On my journey I have
encountered many such women, struggling to recover a
forgotten sense of Spirit, an immediacy and inclusiveness
obscured by patriarchal religious forms. Feminists such as these
are rewriting the canon and are reclaiming what Sharon V. Betcher
refers to as a forgotten 'theology of wetness':

As Hildegard of Bingen recognised, the Holy Spirit
pours herself out upon all flesh. The spirit's potency is
wet, green and juicy: *viriditas* she called it, greening
power. Inasmuch as, metaphorically speaking, the
world is God's body, then God sweats, bleeds, flows,
cries. (Betcher, 1993:14)

Encountering women's spirituality, what was most striking
to me as a man was the valuing of relationship, mutuality and
intimacy, the need to know the people one worshipped with, to
hear their stories and to share one's own, to build community
by really knowing and caring about one another. In these circles
I found a refreshing sense of hope and possibility, a desire to find
new ways to resolve differences, a willingness to work through

GIFTS OF THE GODDESS

conflict in an open and honest way. Even as a man I found myself caught up in something of the excitement, the sense of radical potential, of a life-enhancing alternative, that feminism and women's spirituality embodied. Nor was this some utopian dreaming, for pervading all this sense of an earthy, embodied spirituality was the sombre awareness of sexual politics, the daily reality of discrimination and oppression.

It was, and still is, extremely uncomfortable to be confronted with the reality of sexism and the global prevalence of male violence. Acknowledging the structural, systemic basis of the oppression of women meant that the struggle for gender justice involved more than simply correcting my individual thoughtlessness and insensitivity. As a man identifying with anti-sexist politics in the 1970s, I came to understand how feeling guilty was just another way of avoiding responsibility and change.

But through feminism's challenging of masculine experience as 'normative', its questioning of some of our deepest assumptions and prejudices, I also came to see that male conditioning is itself not given or 'natural'; that there is often a tremendous violence perpetrated against boys and young men in the name of masculinity. Empathy and tenderness are subtly and savagely deconditioned in each generation. The result is 'hard' men; males imprisoned in tight bodies unable to show affection or vulnerability, using either physical force, clever words or mental strategies to keep our own wild feelings at bay and to control others or put them down.

Women helped me to see the violating limitations of our cultural categories of masculine and feminine; I glimpsed how other cultures imagine more playful forms of the cosmic dance of male and female and of yin and yang qualities within us all. During these years I learnt that women conceptualise spirituality differently from men, and that as a culture we could learn so much from this distinctive feminine voice, so long suppressed. I discovered a different way of seeing and being in the world, a source of wisdom that our threatened world, in its

29

headlong rush to activity, to doing and having and possessing, desperately needs. It was in these circles of women that I first learnt about the need for darkness, for lying fallow, and for times of inwardness. I came to value descent as well as ascent.

Women-led circles gave me a vivid experience of the immanence of God, of the presence of what is most holy here in the tangible, sensual world. From them I internalised the celebration of physicality and incarnation as forms of holiness, and an awareness of our faith journeys as necessarily engendered, articulated through the particular channel of our sexual bodies – however that sexuality is expressed or experienced. One evening at the same Summer Solstice celebration in Scotland I was the only man in a small circle of women, who began to talk about their experiences of giving birth. I shall never forget that evening at Laurieston Hall; sat round the wood-burning stove, having nothing myself to contribute for a couple of hours, feeling so privileged to be able to listen to these women's honest, ordinary experiences of the numinous, the everyday miracle of Life. For me that was a holy moment, a time out of time, about which it feels poetically right to speak of the presence of the Goddess.

Whilst I could add nothing to what was said that night, it was during this same period of my life that I was present at the birth of my first child. Here I came directly in touch with incarnational mystery and power. It was a holy, awesome moment, an upsetting inbreaking of the Unspeakable that filled me with wonderment and gratitude, that silenced for a while the chattering of my self-absorption. As our son entered the world I was confronted in a flash with the unfaced terrors of my own mortality; in the light of that mundane miracle I saw the unworthiness of my personal obsessions and ambitions. God was here in the very mess of life, the extremity of physical pain and bodily endurance. Any God worthy of the name could not be apart from all this.

But I was about to experience the first profound crisis of my life. With hindsight it is easy to see that our youthful marriage had no roots; it was grounded in neither the support of family nor faith. We had no 'court of appeal', no place to be held when we encountered the inevitable difficulties of relationship, which were amplified once we had a child. Besides, it was a marriage of its time, when boundaries were blurred, and fidelity was one of the values that 'children of the sixties' called into question. It was a union that was to haemorrhage fatally because both of us failed in the commitment and containment needed. The 1970s marked the high-water mark of the second wave of the Women's Liberation Movement in this country, and looking back I can say, without self-pity or blame, that my first marriage was one of its casualties – or, more honestly, that the truth of feminism was a rock on which it foundered.

Three and a half years after the birth of my son, with the ending of my first marriage and separation from my child, my world seemed to fall apart. At the time I was totally absorbed simply coping day by day. My sense of divinity could not help me in my grief; the Goddess I had come to know was not an entity to intervene in response to my prayers. The priority for me was to address my pain, to explore the territory of my inner world. At the time I did not realise that this would be a vital step on my spiritual journey.

4 Body, self and soul

> We cannot move forward spiritually unless we are also
> willing to deal completely with our personal psychology,
> especially developmental issues from early childhood
> that pattern the way we perceive and react to the present.
> (Bragdon, 1990:3)

As my first marriage fell apart I felt completely lost and
overwhelmed. I had no language to describe what was happening,
no awareness of the psychological patterns which had
contributed to the break-up of what I had thought was the
most important thing in my life. I had no inkling of the vast
subterranean lava flows of the unconscious mind. But with
the loss of certainty and self-confidence I was open to new
understanding.

A friend introduced me to co-counselling, a peer therapeutic
process where equal time is exchanged and in the security of
someone else's non-judgemental attention dammed-up feelings
can be safely felt and released. As past hurts are 'discharged' in
this way, one is able to think more clearly in the here and now.
I learnt that feelings are to be felt and are not a reliable basis
for decisions or action. It was a small step on a long, often
challenging, sometimes joyous journey of self-discovery, one
that took me both inward and back out into the world with
increased awareness.

A few years after the ending of my marriage I went on a men's therapy weekend and was tremendously impressed by the physical energy, the emotional courage and the raw honesty of the leader and participants on the group. Enquiring about the 'model' the leader was using, I discovered Reichian body-based therapy.

In a typical Reichian therapy session, one begins lying on the floor on a mattress with cushions around. As one is encouraged to breathe in a relaxed, continuous way, small movements start to happen spontaneously in different parts of the body. The muscular holding of past hurts, what Wilhelm Reich termed 'body armour', begins to soften, and buried emotions start to be felt.

As one relaxes further and pays attention to these spontaneous movements, 'listening' to them and letting the body be one's guide, the quiet presence of the therapist provides a reassuring 'anchor'; connection is maintained through words, eye-contact or sensitive touch. What happens sooner or later (if it feels safe) is that whatever is being held in the body finds expression. One's whole body may begin to shake or tremble, moving apparently of its own accord. Sobbing and crying, the welling-up of heart-break and sorrow or surprising rage and pent up, congealed anger may pour forth.

But with all this strength of feeling there is a growing awareness of the inner vitality of one's body; pulsations other than the heartbeat may be felt, waves of warmth and a sense of energy streaming through the body are not uncommon. One remembers what it feels like to be wonderfully, totally alive. Once the storms of emotion have passed, feelings of the most all-embracing love often well up. An openness generally follows, a profound sense of peace and communion, of really being in relationship both with the person close by but also, not uncommonly, with humanity at large and with the wider community of life.

Experiencing and training in this work, I discovered its understanding of how we each have an essentially loving, core layer to our being, a place where we feel compassion (literally 'suffer with' others). It is here that we feel both our interconnectedness and our essential individuality. But as we grow up and develop, as we begin to explore the world around us, we encounter inevitable frustrations as well as the shaming and abusive interventions of others (whether deliberate or unintentional). So we develop a secondary level, composed of anger, fear, spite, envy – all pre-verbally, before we can articulate any such feelings. Because we also learn at a very young age that such feelings will not get us the love we crave, we learn to mask these secondary feelings with a veneer, with a socially acceptable mask which we present to the everyday world – this is the third, surface level, the persona of conventional psychology. To be whole is to integrate all three levels and to experience and allow the vital energy of the body to be expressed in appropriate ways. When our basic life-force is denied or suppressed, however, it creates unhealthy rigidities in how we hold our bodies, how we think, even what kind of religion we subscribe to.

Part of what happens as we grow up in the wider culture is that we learn to shut down to our bodies; their wisdom becomes less available to us. In this body-based therapeutic work I gained an insight of great relevance to my spiritual life: I came to appreciate that *truth is actually experienced in the body*, that our bodies are a source of revelation. Our bodies hold stories waiting to be told, and each incarnation is a vehicle for truth. Sadly, in the Christian tradition the body has been seen overwhelmingly as a source of temptation, the site of corruption and decay, an object of contempt or 'benign' neglect.

Bodies are also mistrusted because they are the home to our feelings; in patriarchy emotion is ascribed to women, who are then viewed as somehow unreliable, out of control, given to 'moods'. Yet in my experience my emotions can be an invaluable guide to what is actually happening here and now. To deny them actually puts me in the realm of 'notions', of ideas and fantasies. But our emotions don't come in discrete packets: aliveness is a function of the whole 'system' of my being. If I repress my anger, I stifle my joy; if I deny my grief, I withhold my capacity for empathy and delight.

Through therapy I learnt how what we cannot own in ourselves – whether that is rage, passion, joy or popularity – we project outwards onto others, demonising or idealising them. Yet being *real* with each other involves taking risks – maybe being angry and having the humility to seek reconciliation afterwards. For beneath anger, I found, there is invariably vulnerability, hurt and fear, which the anger conceals. In my experience it is not anger which is the problem but our inability to express it in undamaging ways. Avoiding conflict, hoping never to hurt each other, leads to an increasing shallowness of community life, a polite superficiality that stifles real love and caring.

Theology, for me, remains abstract if it does not include examining and expanding our personal capacity for loving and being loved. Love is an activity not just a feeling, and I have found Scott Peck's definition helpful for this reason: 'The will to extend oneself for the purpose of nurturing one's own or another's spiritual growth' (Peck, 1978:81). In this light I see the body-based therapy I learnt in these years as a kind of 'somatic theology', a way of dealing with the body-memories which stop us being fully present to reality, fully alive to the Presence of God in the here and now, the revelation of truth through the vehicle of our bodies. Sometimes what we most need is this kind of emotional healing rather than some overtly 'spiritual' practice which may actually be a way of the ego remaining in control, of using techniques (of breathing or posture or prayer) by which we actually avoid the truth which is trying to emerge within us.

Therapy taught me to acknowledge the many levels and dimensions of existence. I discovered that the 'spiritual' is not something other-worldly but a deepening appreciation of the sacredness, the miraculousness of the present moment. Sometimes the best spiritual accompanying is to silently give permission for the tears to flow, to simply bear witness to the other person's reality for a moment. Of course therapeutic work, though liberating, often involves a painful journey, which it takes real courage to pursue. In long-term therapy we often have to enter the territory of darkness, the sometimes frightening realm of loss and ending, the place of not-knowing and uncertainty, which is also the ground of germination and birth.

Through my own inner work I experienced the real miracle of incarnation; I encountered directly the mystery of our vital embodiment. Here I had to face the challenge of being real, of discovering the authentic self behind the masks. Confronting the ways I pretend to be what I am not was itself a spiritual discipline. It reminded me of the tale from the Hasidic tradition of Rabbi Zusya, who said, a short while before his death: 'In the world to come I shall not be asked: "Why were you not Moses?" I shall be asked: "Why were you not Zusya?"' (Buber, 1966:17).

What I learnt on this path of personal development was respect for true individuality, which is quite distinct from the individualism of our age. I have found that my selfishness, my tendency to look out only for my own narrow interests, is *always* a symptom of not being in touch with or trusting the compassionate core of my being or that same place in those around me. Self-interest takes over when I do not trust that my true needs will be met.

In his book *The Hungry Spirit*, Charles Handy speaks of 'proper selfishness' as the 'search for ourselves that, paradoxically, we often pursue best through our involvement with others'. To be properly selfish, he suggests, is to 'accept a responsibility for making the most of oneself by, ultimately, finding a purpose beyond and bigger than oneself' (Handy, 1997:9). From such a place one can then open to the spiritual challenge of *self-forgetting*, of losing oneself in service to others in a way that does not patronise them and does not ignore one's own needs and limitations. True humility means a fearless, honest acceptance of who we are, an acknowledgement of our strengths as well as our weaknesses.

The true meaning of sacrifice (*sacreficere*) is to 'make sacred'; it is about giving up what is not essential (not 'of the essence') so that something more genuinely fulfilling, more truthful, can take its place. Sacrifice is actually about choice, about proper discernment, about having the right priorities. Women have taught me that God does not ask us to abandon ourselves; rather we are invited to come home, to love our neighbour *as ourselves*. The challenge then is self-love and self-respect without 'self-exultation', to use John Woolman's phrase.

Through therapy I learnt that transcendence means rising above the narrow identification of Self with personality rather than violent self-negation, as so much of religion has construed it. It means balancing self-love and self-respect with concern for others. That seems to be a timely lesson for our age, as people realise that compassion has to include ourselves. Perhaps this explains why the words of Marianne Williamson (used by Nelson Mandela in his inaugural speech) have struck such a deep chord with many people:

> Our deepest fear is not that we are inadequate. Our deepest fear is that we are powerful beyond measure. It is our light, not our darkness, that most frightens us. We ask ourselves, Who am I to be brilliant, gorgeous, talented, fabulous? Actually, who are you *not* to be? You are a child of God. Your playing small doesn't serve the world. There's nothing enlightened about shrinking so that other people won't feel insecure around you. We are all meant to shine, as children do. We were born to make manifest the glory of God that is within us. It's not just in some of us; it's in everyone. And as we let our own light shine, we unconsciously give other people permission to do the same. As we're liberated from our own fear, our presence automatically liberates others. (Williamson, 1992:165)

Paying attention to our inner, psychological life can, of course, be an indulgence. But I have come to experience more and more the inseparability of the inner and outer worlds; if we wish the world to become loving and compassionate we must become so ourselves, and to diminish fear and prejudice we must address our own. For insofar as we project our power onto others, the political world is only the psychological realm writ large. Journeying beyond our personal defences expands our possibilities and makes us more available for relationships with other people and with our God. Facing ourselves with honesty, seeing the nature of our personality and seeing its limitations, taking responsibility for our feelings of hurt and anger, choosing to change – all these are, in fact, crucial steps to creating world peace.

Once, during a ten-day intensive workshop with Joanna Macy in Cumbria, we were encouraged to go out and practise our listening skills by knocking on people's doors and asking them to name their concerns for the future. All we were to do was listen; we were not to prompt them in any way. We went out in small groups into the backstreets of Barrow-in-Furness, a 'one-company' town, where the Vickers shipyards and their Trident submarines literally dominated the landscape.

That evening we reported back on how it had felt to listen to complete strangers tell us about the pain of our world. I had knocked on the door of an ex-serviceman whose wife had left him just that week, who was feeling absolutely despairing and who claimed to have a gun upstairs in the house. It was an extraordinary discipline to just listen; what we were doing was neither simply therapeutic nor was it political. It was social action based on the spiritual premise of our interconnectedness, our common existence and our relationship to one another at the deepest, most essential level.

Joanna Macy spoke of forms of social witness based on what she described as 'the greening of the self', a shift in identification whereby we remember that:

there is a deep, deep kinship in us, beneath the outer layers of the neocortex or what we learned in school. There is a deep wisdom, a bondedness with our creation, and an ingenuity far beyond what we think we have. (Macy, 1991:192)

Joanna Macy placed this sense that we are all part of a larger, self-corrective system of relationships, a vast field of interlocking processes, in the context of modern science – in particular, systems theory – but it actually mirrors some of humankind's oldest spiritual wisdom. It was this religious awareness that was to occupy me most in subsequent years.

5 All my relations

Who is our neighbour: the Samaritan? the outcast? the enemy? Yes, yes, of course. But it is also the whale, the dolphin and the rain forest. Our neighbour is the entire community of life, the entire universe. We must love it all as our self. (Brian Patrick quoted in Johnson, 1993:67)

On one of her workshops Joanna Macy illustrated what she meant by interdependence by asking us to focus our awareness on the soundwaves of her voice leaving her mouth, travelling across the room and vibrating against our eardrums. She then challenged us to define where 'she' ended and 'we' began. As we drew breath, she invited us to be conscious of the membranes of our lungs, exchanging molecules with the air inside them. What is the point at which the 'air' is in 'us' or 'we' are separate from the 'air'? She invited us to realise that as we breathe we are participating in a vast planetary exchange with all other beings. Rather than supposing we are drawing breath, is it not as accurate to suggest we are being breathed by Life?

Every atom in this body existed before organic life emerged 4,000 million years ago. Remember our childhood as minerals, as lava, as rocks? ... We are the rocks dancing ... It is they that are the immortal part of us. (Seed *et al.*, 1988:36)

At such gatherings, where we were invited to 'awaken to our deep ecology' – an experiential rather than an intellectual process – we often began with an evocation of the 'Beings of the Three Times'. Together we would invoke the beings of the past, inviting their presence into our deliberations, taking time to speak the names of ancestors and teachers, people who had inspired us who were no longer physically present. Then we named those living now who were not in this circle, with whom we share this time of danger and possibility. In the third evocation, calling on the beings of the future times, there was silence; for we do not know their names. That silence was incredibly potent, for the unborn are countless and we are the guardians of their potential, yet we so seldom give them any thought at all.

Such deceptively simple exercises opened up for me a truly religious awareness of *belonging*, of being connected with others, an intrinsic part of a cosmic evolutionary process. Thich Nhat Hanh illustrates this understanding in a story told by one of his students:

One day he showed her a piece of paper. 'Do you see this paper?' he asked.

'Yes,' she replied.

'Look deeply into it. Do you see the logger who cut down the tree to make this piece of paper?'

'Yes. Without him the paper would not be here.'

'Do you see the wife of the logger who made his lunch the day he cut down the tree?'

'Yes.'

'Do you see the truck that hauled the logs? The petrol in the truck? The plants that died millennia ago to form the oil that made the petrol?'

'Yes.'

'Look deeply. Is there anything that is not included in this piece of paper?' (Caldwell, 1996:173)

The week after the Chernobyl nuclear melt-down I was in Norway, where my work took me up onto a glacier, the first time I had visited such a landscape. After leaving the car and walking for some distance out onto the pristine snowfield I came across a pool of startling blue water inside a small ice cave that looked so utterly pure but which my mind warned me would probably be dangerously contaminated. In spite of what I knew I knelt down and washed my hands and face in that glacial water. Perhaps I was being foolish; certainly I felt defiant. I knew deep in my heart that my long-term survival was intimately tied up with that of this small body of water, that its health, its wholeness, and mine were ultimately linked.

It was at about this time that I first heard Matthew Fox, then a Dominican scholar and teacher, who had been invited to speak at St James's Church, Piccadilly, by the rector, Donald Reeves. I found Fox an inspiring preacher, clearly a man with a sense of mission and a great gift to entertain and inform his audience. At St James's his inspiration and enthusiasm were contagious. Combining insights from modern physics and cosmology with the mystical insights of Hildegard of Bingen and Meister Eckhart, Fox spreads the good news that our birthright is to be part of a vast mysterious evolutionary unfolding, that we are all 'royal persons in the kingdom and queendom of God'. His passion and enthusiasm reminded me of all that had been missing from the religion of my schooldays. Fox's map of 'the four paths of Creation-Centred Spirituality' added to Eckhart's *Via Positiva* and *Via Negativa* a third spiritual path, the *Via Creativa*, emphasising the continuity between God's Creation and our own creative nature. But as human creativity can as readily give birth to evil, Fox also conceived of the *Via Transformativa*, the path of justice-making, of action to transform the world, to realise the reign of God on earth. Exploring this map led me into new spiritual territory and I started to discover that what I had experienced in women's circles and in the work with Joanna Macy might be found within the tradition of my childhood.

Following Eckhart – 'every creature is a word of God' (Fox, 1996:122) – Matthew Fox preached that 'the killing of Mother Earth in our time is the number one ethical, spiritual and human issue of our planet' (Fox, 1988:145). He spoke of 'the crucified earth' – seeing the polluted, denatured planet as the most potent, living symbol of the Christ for this generation. He passionately evoked the sense of the Cosmic Christ – the 'divine in every being', the incarnate aspect of God that puts itself at risk by entering fully into physical life. The audaciousness of his vision, the life-affirming sensual-celebratory nature of this spirituality is captured in a poem by one of his colleagues at the Institute of Creation-Centred Spirituality, which he founded and which brought together artists, scientists, theologians and liturgists:

> Christ's blood is green in the branches, blue in the violet.
> Her bright voice laughs in the night wind.
> The big nova swells in her breast.
> Christ suckles us with spring sap and spreads earth under our feet.
> O she loves us, feeds us, tricks us with her triple ways: calls us soul, calls us body, and spirit.
> Calls us to her bed.
> (Richards, 1990)

Hearing Matthew Fox, I felt the same excitement, the same sense of immediate comprehension and identification, of 'convincement' that I imagined happening when people heard early Friends speak. I experienced a profound 'Yes' within my whole body, as if he was articulating something I had known for a very long time deep within me. Like George Fox in his day, Matthew Fox enthusiastically proclaims that 'the Kingdom is already here, it *is* among us!' (Fox, 1991:17). Here, within the walls of St James's, I sensed the possibility for the renewal of religion itself.

One of Fox's colleagues, the Catholic cultural historian Thomas Berry (who describes himself as a 'geologian') speaks of us now entering the 'ecozoic' era of evolution. Now three principles must be recognised: the universe is a communion of subjects, not a collection of objects; the universe is a single sacred community; the human is derivative and the planet is primary. From these it follows that the first purpose of human activity – for instance medicine or economics – is to take care of the health of, or preserve the integral economy of, the planet (Jensen, 1995:39).

What I experienced both in the work with Joanna Macy and in the inspiration of Matthew Fox was a sense of ecology not as science, as knowledge in my mind, but ecology as a re-membering, a restoring of humanity to its rightful place in the universe. And this, I came to appreciate, is an essential task of religion in our age. Rather than simply trying to add some 'green' awareness to our human-centred religious faith, we need to respond to the abundance and essential blessing of creation as a clarion call to wonderment and thanksgiving which can inspire and sustain our work for justice and peace. Awareness of our interdependence invites us to respect all forms of life, not because we give them economic value or find them beautiful, but because of their intrinsic worth within the diversity of the sacred whole:

Woven into our lives is the very fire from the stars and the genes from the sea creatures, and everyone, utterly everyone, is kin in the radiant tapestry of being. (Johnson, 1993:39)

This takes us beyond the notion of 'stewardship', which, as Elizabeth A. Johnson points out, 'misses the crucial aspect of human dependence on that which we steward'.

The very word 'environmentalism' betrays our human-centredness, as Marshall Massey of Intermountain Yearly Meeting explains:

When I say 'global ecosystem' I identify it as the web of all life, in which every thread is equally a part of the whole; and when I say 'Creation' I identify it as the whole of what God made, in which every bit is equally the child of God's love. But when I say 'the environment' I define it as what surrounds (environs) me. I am the player, it is my stage: the same misconception yet again. (Massey, 1989:53)

Restoring a sense of sacred ecology, of our belonging to the earth, is one of the most exciting spiritual challenges of our age. The explosion of interest in aboriginal and earth-centred spiritual traditions – with books and courses on Native American medicine wheel teachings, shamanism and earth mysteries abounding – testifies to the deep hunger and alienation from the earth that people in our culture feel. ('All my relations' is the prayer said on entering a sweat lodge, a Native American purification ceremony.)

What is emerging today is nothing less than a new recognition of an ancient sense of covenant – not between a tribal God and 'his' people but one between humanity and the commonwealth of Life. 'Green' spirituality is pre-eminently about addressing questions of meaning and value and challenging what Mark Burch perceptively calls our 'consumptive lifestyle' (Burch, 1995:7). Materialism is actually a misnomer: we do not value, let alone reverence, matter. Once again it was women who taught me to value the commonplace and the mundane, who taught me that what is right in front of us is no less miraculous for being plentiful. Alice Walker speaks of how: 'We alone can devalue gold by not caring whether it rises or falls in the market place ... feathers, shells, and sea-shaped stones are all as rare. This could be our revolution: to love what is plentiful as much as what is scarce.'

Elizabeth A. Johnson regards what is crucial for a viable future as 'a religious spirit that converts us to the earth'; she sees that we all, women and men alike, 'need to fall in love with the earth as an inherently valuable, living community in which we participate, and be creatively faithful to it' (Johnson, 1993:62). If we are to rise to this challenge, we need fresh spiritual resources, reclaimed symbols and imagery; we need to develop appropriate forms of worship and liturgy and imaginatively rewrite the holy texts:

> Helped are those who love the Earth, their mother, and who willingly suffer that she may not die; in their grief over her pain they will weep rivers of blood, and in their joy in her lively response to love, they will converse with trees ...

> Helped are those who find the courage to do at least one small thing each day to help the existence of another – plant, animal, river, human being. They shall be joined by a multitude of the timid.

> Helped are those who lose their fear of death; theirs is the power to envision the future in a blade of grass.

> Helped are those who love and actively support the diversity of life; they shall be secure in their differentness.

> Helped are those who know.

> 'The Gospel according to Shug' (Walker, 1989:288-9)

6 Ritual and re-membering

The purpose of ritual is to wake up the old mind, to put it to work. The old ones inside us, the collective unconscious, the many lives, the different eternal parts, the senses and the parts of the brain that have been ignored. Those parts do not speak English. They do not care about television. But they do understand candlelight and colours. They do understand nature.

(Z. Budapest quoted in Carnes & Craig, 1998:93)

In order to enter the low domed structure of a sweat lodge you have to get down on all fours; you prostrate yourself. I find it a beautiful gesture of humility, a physical reminder that 'humus' and 'humility' come from the same linguistic root, that by staying close to the ground we won't go far wrong. Through the smell of the damp earth my animal senses are awakened and as I enter this place of utter darkness and free myself of all outside stimulus, I am choosing to encounter the Unknown. I am entering a ritual space that symbolises both the darkness of the womb and that of the grave.

When everyone is seated in a silent circle, rocks that have been heated in a fire nearby until they are white hot are passed into the darkness and placed in a pit in the centre of the sweat lodge. Herbs are sprinkled on them as prayers are said. Water is added and the heat and humidity roll over my body in waves. It is an intense, physical experience of prayer, the heat driving out any thoughts, opinions or judgements. Only the present moment is real. At times I feel I am going to die; I know I cannot stay in a moment longer. But this fear passes; I bend lower for the air I have been told is slightly cooler near the ground.

The sweat lodge is like a sacred sauna, but it is also different for its intimate contact with the earth, the utter darkness, the surrender of ordinary consciousness that it calls for. Traditionally there are four cycles of prayers (prayers for others, for ourselves, for our world and a final, silent round of waiting for vision, for guidance, for a sense of direction), between each of which there is a pause and a chance to leave the circle. Afterwards it is customary to immerse oneself in water, preferably in a river or stream. The feeling of deep cleansing is extraordinary. Physically, emotionally and spiritually there is a sense of great release. Of course, like any living ritual form, it's a different experience every time, and each sweat lodge is only as prayerful as those who lead and participate in it. Like Quaker meeting, every one I've been in has had its own character.

*   *   *

Such a sweat lodge has been built beside a fast-flowing mountain stream in Snowdonia. Here a group of men have gathered for six days for an event I helped to devise called 'Men's Rites of Passage'. The group has already spent three days telling their stories, making camp together, working side by side and building trust in one another. Now they have been invited to create meaningful rituals to mark and honour unfinished transitions in their lives. These rituals, we have explained, are not something imposed or fixed but something we will create together as a group. The rituals will be made up of elements and symbols that have meaning for the individual, that derive from the life journey each man has described at length. Telling their stories the participants have shared tears and anger, joy and humour. Now we have entered a different arena, a space in which archetypal energies will be at work, where mountain stream, moonlight or the dying embers of the fire will play their part as potent symbols of what cannot be put into words.

We enter liminal space together, literally crossing a threshold, choosing to take time apart from our everyday lives so that we can open to a different awareness. By ritual we mean a body-based encounter with something vaster and older than what we can see and name, the spiritual reality that is at once both within and 'beyond' the visible world, a Presence greater even than the mountains, the sky, the sunlight or the myriad tiny creatures parading through the grasses at our feet. Here we are willing to be surprised and challenged by a wisdom none of us possess but any of us may channel.

Each of these rituals is different, tailored to the needs of the participant. Speaking from the heart, finding both support and challenge from other men, participants may hear within them a 'voice' they do not usually own. As their hearts open, once fear and frustration and judgement and anger have been named and given expression, an extraordinary quality of truth-telling, of *authenticity* begins to emerge. Men show their affection openly for one another, they rediscover their capacity to nurture, they overcome their fear of one another and become more real. By creating such rituals we re-member who we are, we feel an integrity of mind-body-spirit.

Men have traditionally gone into wilderness as pioneers, as hunters and as conquering armies. Here we are in nature to listen, to seek instruction, to recall being part of an essential Mystery, a greater body, of which we are just one tiny cell. Here we can put our life-decisions in proper perspective and glimpse a different kind of masculinity. Once each man has told us about himself – both consciously in words and unconsciously through the way he is in the group – the rest of us prepare a ritual using the elements or life situation that has been identified. The element of surprise is important; the individual is always free to refuse what he is offered, but to be surprised we each have to step beyond our personal control of the situation. What we devise may involve both physical and emotional challenge. Some men need to confront denial, to face their grief or to accept more responsibility; some need to learn to accept tenderness and affection, to open to the trust and nurturing of other men; others need to explore their physical power and courage. Each ritual tends to be, unsurprisingly, the very opposite of what men *thought* they wanted.

This work with men grew out of the 'deep ecology' explorations with Joanna Macy. On one of her intensive workshops she asked if there was a particular 'constituency' we felt led to work with and I knew at once that for me it was working with men, working to heal the ways we are cut off from nature – both from the earth and from the realms of feeling and inner knowing. Seeing what men in positions of temporal power were doing unawarely meant that the healing of men and the healing of our planet were inseparable for me. Soon after that three of us, with backgrounds in therapy, storytelling and anthropology, created this form which we called 'Men's Rites of Passage'.

Traditionally part of what is taught in ceremonies and rituals is the culture's cosmology. Here the individual learns their place within the greater story of their people and their people's kinship with the rest of life on earth. We wanted to contradict the masculine conditioning that teaches men to be out of touch with their own deep self and incapable of authentic intimacy with others. By incorporating elements of storytelling, music and therapy with the experience of being in nature, we found this gave men permission for a great creative outpouring, for celebration and playfulness, for real humour and healing. The emphasis was always on following the energy in the present moment, not forcing anything but sensing the truth that was right here and now (not even that of a minute ago). The focus of the group would shift from person to person, staying with whatever was truly most alive; we 'allowed' chaos as several things might be happening at once. But we trusted that there was always an authentic process trying to unfold, if only we could discern it. Sometimes this involved silent waiting, sometimes furious physical activity; occasionally it involved physical challenge or endurance (although given men's tendency to bravado this was the least likely form for it to take). It was exhilarating and exhausting, and required a tremendous focus of attention to stay with what was happening, to notice the sparks of Life suddenly flickering at the periphery of our vision.

These rituals were something created by a temporary community who had laughed and cried together, taken risks and really been present for each other physically and emotionally. These were extraordinarily vivid and colourful events that have profoundly influenced my sense of spiritual community and the possibilities of worship.

Ever since my involvement in women's spirituality, I had retained a rhythm of observing the festivals of the changing seasons and had remained aware of the lunar cycles as a way of marking times of increase and diminishment. I found myself making simple altars, places to honour the elements of earth, water, fire and air, places decorated with objects of meaning to me, with words or images that helped me to focus my awareness. I would light candles as part of quiet, reflective time.

In other cultures there is the recognition that in a very real sense we are not alone, isolated as human beings in the universe, but are in true and deep communion with other beings. As children we are encouraged to retain this understanding; story-books are full of talking animals and magical happenings. But then we are expected to 'grow up' and leave such foolishness behind, to learn the scientific view that such attitudes are superstitious, to learn to treat the world as inanimate (literally 'without a soul'). Having banished the spirits that once inhabited every corner of the earth, we now depend on human ingenuity to give life meaning. This is one legacy of the

Enlightenment, the heritage of uncertainty and isolation in a dis-spirited world.

In the women's circles, in the 'deep ecology' and creation spirituality groups, and again in the men's work, ritual was a common thread. And it has become central to my understanding of faith. For faith is so much more than belief; the courage of the faithful is the certainty that we are not alone, that we belong where we are and that there is a pattern to existence from which nothing, not even death, can separate us. Through ritual I have experienced that this pattern is the mystery of life on earth evolving; I am 'held' by this greater whole, I am part of a web I cannot fall out of. My fear of death is only a momentary forgetting of this.

In all times and cultures human beings have used ritual to help us to re-member who we are. Through ritual we re-enact our place in the cosmos and are assisted through the difficult transitions of personal and social life by the invisible spiritual forces we invoke at such times. Ritual, when it is alive, when the participants are involved in a meaningful and creative way, is an essential human activity, a way of containing our necessary but terrifying encounter with the Mystery at the heart of life. It is the human vehicle for encounters with the numinous; it offers a tried and tested containment for that meeting, a means to lose our selves and yet return safely to the everyday world afterwards. The basic impulse is to seek *ekstasis* (literally 'being out of place') and in the absence of meaningful ritual (and in the face of other pressures in their lives) growing numbers of young people turn to chemical substitutes for genuine transcendent experience. But today there is once more a growing interest in meaningful ritual; people are inventing new forms to express and fulfil this human need.

One of the ironies of my spiritual journey is that just as I was most actively exploring these creative forms of ritual I also found myself led among Friends, whose position on outward sacraments and ritual forms was early on expressed by William Penn:

> This world is a form. Our bodies are forms. And no visible acts of devotion can be without forms. But yet the less form in religion the better, since God is a spirit. For the more mental our worship, the more adequate to the nature of God; the more silent, the more suitable to the language of a spirit. Words are for others, not for ourselves. Nor for God, who hears not as bodies do, but as spirits should. (Penn quoted in Bonner, 1993:59f)

To earlier generations of Friends the rejection of outward forms depended on a collective experience of the inner Christ as the 'presence in the midst' at the heart of their meetings, guiding all present, leading them into unity under that single leadership. But is that our common experience now? Can we today agree about the Presence that guides us? Does Quaker worship still depend on this shared sense of a living Presence? Today individual Friends in Britain Yearly Meeting may also attend Eucharist in other churches, go on Buddhist retreats, practise yoga and various forms of meditation – clearly there is something they find elsewhere that they are not getting from meeting for worship. Does it matter that just as we acknowledge that silent worship is not for everyone it seems we tacitly accept that it may also not be the only form of worship for any one of us? What is the meaning of Quaker silence today?

I have found myself wondering if the absence of outward forms and symbols is *essential* to Quaker worship. Nowadays we seem to think of the value of Quaker plainness of worship as lying in the fact that in the silence and absence of symbols none are offended and none need feel excluded. But this is a very different basis to silent worship than the dynamic and transforming process early Friends described: their worship depended on something more fundamental than mere silence, it *followed on from* the process of 'turning to the Light'. That was the basis of the power of their ministry.

Outward sacraments and symbols can, however, actually convey and instill in people something of the *fleshiness* of religion, which Quaker worship too often lacks (a point made to me by Timothy Peat, who has experience of both the Catholic priesthood and the ways of Friends). Paradoxically, without outward forms and without this sensual level of religious observance, there is a danger of us becoming purely cerebral in our worship, of our faith becoming heady and ultimately purely *notional* – the very thing early Friends railed against. There is today a real danger that, without the experience of power in our meetings, we make an idolatry of silence, a formalism of the absence of forms. As Rufus Jones reminded Friends, 'Silence itself has no magic' (Gorman, 1979:41).

The key element of meeting for worship is not silence; it is stilling our busy selves (what the Buddhists call the monkey mind, our frantic little egos) and expectantly *waiting*. The ways we might then express the truth which is revealed to us could be many and various. We are accustomed, we have come to assume, that the only legitimate response to divine prompting is (generally rather sombre) spoken ministry. But what if this process of stilling ourselves and hearing the leadings of God is aided as much by the sincere *and appropriate* use of symbols as it is by silence? Can Quaker worship legitimately include body prayer (movement and dance) or the use of symbols or images *if these have authentic life for the worshipper at that time?*

> Ritual consists of the external practices of spirituality that help us become more receptive and aware of the closeness of our lives to the sacred. Ritual is the act of sanctifying action – even ordinary actions – so that it has meaning: I can light a candle because I need the light or because the candle represents the light I need. (Baldwin, 1990:163)

Harvey Gillman described to me an autumn weekend at Charney Manor, during which for the Sunday meeting for worship Friends brought in leaves and berries and natural symbols of the changing season, creating in effect a spontaneous 'harvest festival'. Harvey said that this felt deeply 'in the Life' on that occasion. The danger he could foresee was if Friends tried to institutionalise this and started to plan to do the same thing again the following year! It seems to me vital that we maintain our testimony against times and seasons to prevent us from falling into the trap of thinking we can dictate certain forms in advance of a given occasion. But that doesn't mean that we shouldn't be more experimental in our worship. Indeed, I would say we are called upon to worship adventurously at all times rather than succumbing to 'celebrating' harvest-time or Christmas or Easter or any fixed festivals in outward forms *if they do not have life for us.*

I remember being part of one of the morning 'experimental worship groups' at the Lancaster Summer Gathering in 1995. Giving ourselves permission to explore meeting for worship in new ways, we met outside among the trees and birdsong, we spent one morning silently washing one another's hands in a circle, and we found one day that the ministry of truth was to hear one Friend telling of her difficulties with her meeting and why she felt she had to resign her membership. Each of these hours was different, and each felt charged with Life, with authenticity, with the liberating potential of waiting and being led in the moment, of truth arising in that time and place and moving us into deeper communion, into more authentic relationship with one another and with the sacred circle of Life. The group felt empowering as we took risks together, as we were vulnerable to one another, as we answered that of God in one another.

Permitting this kind of genuine, surprising spontaneity seems an essential component of Quakerism to me. I remember in the early 1980s spending time in London with Fran Peavey, the American social change activist. After an evening meal together I asked Fran what her plans were. She said she would know in the morning; she would either fly on to India to visit the Ganges Reclamation Project she was involved in, or she would go home to San Francisco. I didn't know at the time that

Fran was a Quaker; all I knew was that I had never met a
person so alive to the guidance of the Spirit in the moment.
Her openness and trust highlighted my own sense of caution and
control, subtly illuminating the underlying reality of my fear.
Something in Fran 'answered' the fear in me without anything
being said aloud.

Her trust in her own discernment reminded me of James
Nayler that morning at the plough when he received the call
and promptly left his work and family, or of Simon and his
brother Andrew casting aside their nets to follow Jesus as
'fishers of men'. Is this not how we should be living – able to
respond to the promptings of the Spirit as they arise? (Of
course, faithfulness means discerning the call to stay put as
much as to move on, as we are led.)

This question of spontaneity makes me wonder how much
we fall into patterns in our worship. How often do we feel
moved to minister in joyous thanksgiving, adoration or an
uninhibited sense of celebration in our worship? Thankfully we
have come a long way from earlier generations of Friends who
were inhibited by the Puritan denial of pleasure and the arts, of
the joy of human imagination. Most Friends today greatly
value the enrichment that creativity of all kinds can bring; so
what if we allowed ourselves to be more experimental and
imaginative in our worship; what if we let the flower of Quaker
simplicity be fertilised by the immediacy of divine inspiration
so that our worship could blossom into new life?

Ritual need not be complex or theatrical; it is mainly a
matter of intention, an attitude of mind and body, an attention
to detail and a mindfulness of movement and speech. I
remember a circle of Friends in the Quiet Room at Woodbrooke
passing round a stone and a feather and describing the things
we felt burdened by and the things we carried lightly. It was an
example of what Matthew Fox refers to as 'intermediate ritual'
– not ritual as fixed form, like a church service imposed on a
congregation led by one or two clergy, but rather ritual as an
expression of community, a heartfelt utterance of an all too

human need. Friends, with our lack of dogma and liturgical tradition, are well placed to play a part in empowering people to move beyond dependence on priests and set liturgical forms towards a trusting and creative expression of the human need for meaningful ritual.

Of course, to depart from our customary form of Quaker worship would require us to be even more diligent in our discipline of discernment; we would have to listen well to the place 'where words come from'. But we should remember that this much-loved phrase came to us from a people who were holding ceremonies and councils for many generations before Quakers appeared in the Americas. Can we today, if we are confident of the basis of our silent, unprogrammed tradition, also imagine meetings where the stillness and expectant waiting might lead to song and dance, to a circle of sharing from the heart, or even follow on from the sharing of meaningful symbols (for what are words but symbols anyway)? Or are we too *precious* about our silent meetings, too comfortable with what is familiar, whether there is life and power in it or not?

Many meetings seem now to be expecting everything of one hour on a Sunday morning. In earlier times, however, as well as public meetings for worship to which any were welcome, Friends had threshing meetings, for discussion and teaching, and retired meetings, for more 'seasoned' Friends to deepen in worship together. By all accounts any of these meetings might have lasted for three or four hours. Today, when so many have come to Quakerism either wounded from experiences of imposed religion (and therefore wanting to avoid all mention of God and Christ) or else bringing the baggage of other denominations, might there not be a case for semi-programmed meetings, gatherings at which we explain the Quaker way of worship even while we invite people into experiencing it? Could we benefit from experimenting with new forms, combining Bible study, stillness, movement and spontaneous ministry?

'Ritual' seems to be a word that holds a lot of fear for

modern Friends; either they associate it exclusively with Christian liturgy performed by rote, or else they think it refers to a primitive, superstitious kind of religious observance we have 'of course' left behind. But I have a different experience. Many times I have taken part in an extraordinary process that has some of the hallmarks of a therapeutic process (the grieving, the lamentation, the joyous bodily expression of vitality) but which is also something more, a deep re-membering, a respectful, essentially mysterious process that takes us out of our selves and into the larger body of Life, that encourages us to feel the rhythms and passages of our lives as seasons in an eternal story of growing and renewal, of suffering and release, of grieving, welcoming and letting go. I have been part of such circles on hillsides and in church halls, in meeting houses and community centres. I cannot doubt the power and authenticity of what I have witnessed there and I am heartened when I find myself among Friends who are willing to experiment and to explore such creative forms of worship.

7 Darkness and new life

Our life is love, and peace, and tenderness; and bearing one with another, and forgiving one another, and not laying accusations one against another; but praying one for another, and helping one another up with a tender hand, if there has been any slip or fall; and waiting till the Lord gives sense and repentance, if sense and repentance in any be wanting.
(Penington, 1994:486)

I find it significant that in *Quaker faith & practice* part of this passage is quoted, but the excerpt ends before any mention of slipping or falling. Certainly, one of the things that drew me to Friends was the knowledge that, from the earliest days of the movement, Quakers were known for not 'preaching up sin'. Yet I find myself feeling deprived of a religious language that enables me to name my falling short, a vocabulary for the times when I deny God or, through stubborn pride or arrogant fantasy, isolate myself from the web of life and relationship.

After ten years of attending meeting for worship and meetings for business at all levels, the Quaker sense of 'turning to the Light' still remained mysterious to me. Yet in terms of religious identity I was moving from the eclectic mix of pagan, feminist, spiritual-ecological explorations I have been describing, towards a more solid identification of myself as a

Quaker – albeit bringing these influences with me, and doubtless trying to tailor Quakerism to fit my motley cloth. I still didn't think of myself as any kind of Christian. In this I could find comfort in the Quaker belief that it is not what we 'profess' that matters but how we live our lives. But I was still sensing that there was more to my resistance than this.

Knowing that, for all my self-directed reading, I was still painfully ignorant of Quaker tradition, I was grateful for a bursary to study at Woodbrooke for the autumn term of 1994. What I only dimly realised at the time was that to appreciate Quakerism I would need to be open to its Christian roots (and that to make sense of Christianity one must explore its Jewish origins!). Thanks to further bursary support, I stayed at Woodbrooke for three terms and still knew I was only scratching the surface. What happened to me during that year, however, was something which I later discovered was not at all uncommon. Going to Woodbrooke ostensibly to study Quaker tradition, I was both making space in my life and putting myself in the sensitive care of people who would hold me through what was to be a painful life-transition, an experience that was to take me to the heart of the very thing that (with my mind) I was trying to comprehend.

I would not have been open to what was about to happen to me, however, without several other leadings along the way. Carrying the 'baggage' I did from childhood, I came among Friends 'allergic' to things overtly Christian. I had great difficulty hearing Bible stories or anything that for me meant religious indoctrination. But amongst Friends I found my resistance gradually being eroded, like a stone worn smooth by successive tides. This healing process began subtly once I made the commitment to this community, once I signalled a sincere intention to follow this path.

A decisive moment occurred many years earlier when I was living in a Quaker-inspired intentional community in east London. One of my lovers at the time was herself a Friend, and we were both attending one of Joanna Macy's workshops at a venue near Bath. During a period of free time she said, 'There's somewhere I have to take you near here.' So we borrowed a car and set off to I knew not where. Told where to drive, told when to park, and told in which direction to walk through a small market town I had never visited before, I trustingly found myself in the centre of Bradford-on-Avon.

My partner had known only that she was led to take me to Bradford-on-Avon's Saxon chapel, but we had arrived at dusk and quite expected the building to be locked. To our surprise it wasn't, but once inside we couldn't find a light-switch. We felt our way silently around the ancient cold stone walls, slowly discovering the layout of the interior in the pitch dark, and then my companion, her 'work' done, went to sit quietly on one of the pews. I wandered over to the foot of what would have been the small bell tower and suddenly found myself down on my knees on the stone flag floor. I heard a voice 'say' within me, 'You have to respect what people have honoured in these places.'

Somewhat shaken, not knowing what to make of this, I got up and went to sit next to my partner. As I sat down beside her, almost immediately I got a 'picture' of a wedding ceremony taking place in a small country chapel full of flowers. Shortly afterwards we left the building in silence and as we crossed the car park I said to her in a trembling voice, 'I think we've got to get married.' It was hardly a romantic proposal, more like the recognition of a call to obedience. But so it was that two Quakers – one a Friend from childhood, the other recently joined – married two years later in the Lady chapel of a small rural church, festooned with greenery and flowers left over from a local 'society' wedding.

At the ceremony itself the bride was barefoot, a lamentation for the earth was read and a colleague played the didgeridoo. The theme of the address was trust and promise in a time of uncertainty, the reading was from Matthew: 'Consider the lilies of the field'. We were embarking on a journey without a known destination, but I felt that I had definitely been led to this place, literally and metaphorically. In spite of all that I could not make sense of, in spite of all the fear I felt, I entered wholeheartedly into this commitment – both to my bride and to whatever was leading us; it was to be a triangular relationship! Now I did feel I was coming home, I was coming back to Life; I was making a commitment to turning, to changing direction away from my controlling, rational self. The God I felt present that day was inviting me to surrender, to enter a mystery and to trust beyond anything my conscious mind could grasp. Marriage (especially for those of us who have failed at this commitment previously and know we have to struggle with the vows we have taken) is surely an act of faith, a vocation, and not simply a matter of conscious choice.

Looking back on that visit to the chapel at Bradford-on-Avon, I recall that I was told to *respect* what had been honoured in such places. I was not asked to *believe in* anything. The experience meant, of course, that I had to engage with and question just what it was that people through the ages had honoured in church buildings and religious forms. So when I arrived at Woodbrooke nearly ten years later I brought both my resistance and my willingness to be led in equal measure, but with them both a sense that there was something I needed to articulate and to have threshed out.

At Woodbrooke I enjoyed the mental stimulation of the courses, the luxury of twenty-four-hour access to the wonderful library, the heated (for Friends) discussions over cups of tea. My tutorial relationship with one of the staff soon deepened and assumed an unforeseen importance; it became a precious, unforgettable experience of spiritual direction. I was challenged and upheld in prayer; I felt my spiritual life enriched in a new way – with both the nurturing of the community and this added dimension of one-to-one spiritual accompaniment. Towards the end of my year at Woodbrooke, still basking in the glow of the enthusiasm of the newly converted, I prayed one day 'to have my illusions shattered', so keen was I to get to 'the truth'. My tutor/director pointed out that this was perhaps a rash prayer for a beginner. It was not long before my prayers were answered.

At about this time I did something in my professional life about which I felt deeply ashamed. I found with hindsight that I had violated my own deepest values and hurt someone I cared for and had thought I was helping. For a very long time I was in denial about what I had done – compounding, I realised later, the hurt I had already caused. I rationalised my actions, I tried to put the responsibility for what had happened on other people. I secretly blamed even those marginally involved for not supporting me enough.

It was over a year before I was able to really face what I had done. Gradually I saw how I had lost my integrity and deceived myself and therefore the other person. Realising my mistakes, I fell into a pit of shame and self-recrimination. I became obsessive in my self-chastisement, while being consumed by fear of the consequences of my actions. I stopped working altogether, no longer trusting my own judgement. I tried to pray, but even my prayers seemed filled with self-pity. The more I tried, the further I seemed from any sense of God. I felt myself abandoned and unworthy because I *had* indeed done wrong. I lost all confidence in my own discernment, for I had thought I was acting with integrity, was doing something truly inspired and 'of God'. But I came to realise that there are powerful, deceiving impulses within, forces far more treacherous and much more beguiling than my conscious will or stated intentions. I had to face my own capacity for sin.

Until this episode I had no sense of ever having done anything more than make fairly easily correctable mistakes. Now I was slowly being forced to examine whole areas of my life that I wasn't proud of. Soon it became clear that rather than being about one particular, if considerable, lapse of judgement – which I could rationalise away – what was being revealed to me was a broader picture of how I pretend to be what I am not, how I give the impression of knowing more than I do, and how I fail to ask for or be really open to help and support – the many ways, in fact, in which 'I' try to remain in charge and 'go it alone' in my life. All of which are examples, of course, of pride. But this awareness was something for which the self-examination of the therapeutic world (with which I was so familiar) had somehow not prepared me, had even helped me, perhaps, to ignore. What I was forced to recognise was how I 'profess' faithfulness but actually refuse to surrender my life to God, to anything, most of the time, beyond my own ego.

In my desperation and from a sense of mounting crisis, I not only had to ask for others' help (as in my proud, self-confident times I saw no need to), I also started to beseech God to help me through each sleepless night; I began to pray an unfamiliar, desperate kind of prayer, like a child in pain. I experienced first hand poverty of spirit and the compassion it elicits.

At the time I found it almost impossible to share my difficulties with members of my meeting (even with my fellow elders). I was ashamed and embarrassed to admit the exact circumstances of what I had done, but I also felt the absence of both the trust in *and the degree of distance from* them that I might have felt with an ordained minister in another denomination. Perhaps this was merely further pride on my part, but at this moment of greatest need, the phrase 'the priesthood of all believers' had a very hollow ring. I felt the weakness of our lack of training and preparation for the full dimensions of pastoral care; I wanted something that wasn't counselling (which would seek to make me feel better); I wanted the Quaker equivalent of confession and absolution.

Though at the yearly meeting level I did know Friends with whom I could find spiritual support and counsel, it was a testing time for my identity as a Friend. What I was led to was the Twelve-Step fellowships of those 'recovering' from addictions. Here I found a kind of self-surrender and with it a genuine humility that I was not finding among Quakers. Here was a simplicity of faith born of the experience of lives that had been broken open by dependence on substances or behaviours over which people knew they had no control. In small groups we shared our stories and encouraged one another not to 'slip' (the actual word used for lapses), to live without the substance or behaviour that caused us shame, 'one day at a time'. This process included the sense of confessional I needed at the time and it taught me how sobriety refers to far more than abstaining from alcohol.

Here I met others who readily admitted they had done things they were ashamed of, who had been brought down enough to admit their total dependence on God as they understood God. In addiction a person isolates themself, acts wilfully and often breaks the trust others have in them. Recovery from an addiction requires a directness, an absolute honesty I found both challenging and refreshing. We were addicts together, supporting each other to hand our lives over completely to God because we had acknowledged we could no longer operate under our own power. Here newcomers were not offered a theology but were given practical steps which, in the experience of those who had gone before, would lead to wholeness.

From these circles I came to understand the truth of Sam Keen's observation that 'The greatest addiction of all is to our personality – our routines, roles, rigidities ... Addiction is the idolatry of the ego' (Keen, 1985:138-9). From my own experience of 'falling short' and from the process of taking a searching personal 'moral inventory' (one of the Twelve Steps devised by the original recovery fellowship of Alcoholics Anonymous), I came to acknowledge just how impatient, critical, envious and controlling I can be. I had to face the many forms my greed takes – some socially acceptable (such as my compulsion to acquire knowledge, to indulge my obsession with buying books) and others less so (such as my lust, which is a corruption of true sexual desire).

Addiction, I learnt, cannot be confined, if we are honest, to the ghetto of those who are dependent on so-called 'hard drugs'. Competition, striving, stress, work, excitement, status, food, sex, romance – not to mention alcohol, tobacco, sugar and prescribed medicines – can all be dependences that alter our mood and form the basis of 'the tyranny of a false, idolatrous desire' (Keen, 1985:139). Seen in this light, the growing popularity of Twelve-Step programmes can be seen as a way people are seeking to come to terms with what has traditionally been known as sin.

Yet whenever I raised the subject of sin I got very mixed reactions. A Jewish friend saw it as a singularly Christian concern; a feminist theologian saw it as an obsession of men – for women, she argued, what was sinful was failing to fulfil one's potential, failing to assert or look after oneself. Today amongst British Friends you will hardly ever hear the word spoken. But when I try to describe the ways in which we fail to live up to our potential, or when I seek to find language to describe the evil of our destruction of the earth, I need strong language that can describe both our personal and collective 'falling short'. Whilst needing to speak of the experience of sinning, I know the word itself has been corrupted, has inescapable associations with guilt and a theology of personal salvation.

At a recent Quaker Retreat Group gathering at Charney Manor, during an unstructured evening, I asked the other participants if they found the idea of sin at all important or meaningful. I was amazed that what began as a rather diffident enquiry on my part soon turned into a worship-sharing session that lasted an hour and a half and could have gone on for longer. I was heartened to discover that for some Friends at least the word still has a deep resonance. Several personal contributions that evening helped me better to understand my own situation:

Sin is whatever we feel we need to be forgiven for; it is not being in right relationship to God, what early Friends meant by being out of Gospel order. Sin is not taking responsibility (i.e. blaming others) for what has been hurtful or destructive. It is not being true to our real self, the divine part of us, but being caught up in the fallible, human part. It includes malice, thoughtlessness, impulsiveness – always with an element of self-deceit. It is not believing ourselves beloved children of God; George Fox said that sin is denying God's love for us. Sin is not only the big things (murder, rape, theft, etc.) but the times of falseness in relation to others and ourselves. If we think we haven't sinned then we haven't been properly searched by the Inner Light. Sin is any barrier or obstacle between ourselves and the love of God. Recognising our sins means realising that something needs to happen to heal that broken or blocked relationship. Our calling is to be a redemptive community, a people who see the sins of the world and pray for forgiveness for them all. We will be motivated by God's forgiveness to do right in the world, but we have to be redeemed ourselves, so first of all we have to admit our sinning. What we seek is collective redemption, not personal salvation. Real friendship includes challenge and struggle, saying hard things to one another, a commitment to working things through, a process of discerning the truth over time. Saying what is hard takes real courage.

In our reflections we also focused on our specific difficulties as Friends. In the silent confession of a Quaker meeting we do not necessarily express contrition and feel the forgiveness that comes from owning our sin. It is certainly not helpful to be affirmed too soon – 'I'm sure you didn't mean to do it' or 'You'll never do it again'. If we don't properly confess and really feel forgiven then we get stuck in neurotic guilt.

As I struggled to come to terms with my own new-found awareness of sin, I sat in meeting for worship one morning at Woodbrooke, still berating myself, still trying to *understand* what I had done wrong and hoping to find someone to unburden myself to (and yet still feeling ashamed and not wanting to talk about what I had done) – all the things the mind can do to prevent one from merely being present, simply centring down in worship. Suddenly I was filled with an awareness which 'said' to me: 'You *have* done wrong/you are not a bad person'. As I held these two – to my *mind* – contradictory statements in equal balance, I suddenly realised in that moment that God had forgiven me. As I let in the both/and nature of the message, I felt my burden lighten. Later, I found my dawning self-acceptance described by the American poet Mary Oliver:

Wild Geese

You do not have to be good.
You do not have to walk on your knees
for a hundred miles through the desert, repenting.
You only have to let the soft animal of your body
love what it loves.
Tell me about despair, yours, and I will tell you mine.
Meanwhile the world goes on.
Meanwhile the sun and the clear pebbles of the rain
are moving across the landscapes,
over the prairies and the deep trees,
the mountains and the rivers.
Meanwhile the wild geese, high in the clear blue air,
are heading home again.
Whoever you are, no matter how lonely,
the world offers itself to your imagination,
calls to you like the wild geese, harsh and exciting –
over and over announcing your place
in the family of things.

(Oliver, 1986:14)

As I sought to make amends to all those I now realised I had harmed throughout my life, the weight of remorse started to lift and my obsessing about my wrong-doing (which was itself another form of pride) began to diminish. This process continues for me as a daily discipline, noticing my 'slips and falls', making amends where appropriate.

Part of what I learnt from this period of darkness is just how strongly my pride keeps me from really surrendering my life in the way I believe we are called to as Quakers. Through this painful personal experience, the writings of early Friends began to have new life for me:

> Give over thine own willing, give over thine own running, give over thine own desiring to know or be anything and sink down to the seed which God sows in the heart, and let that grow in thee and be in thee and breathe in thee and act in thee; and thou shalt find by sweet experience that the Lord knows and loves and owns that, and will lead it to the inheritance of Life, which is its portion. (Penington, 1661, QFP 26.70)

Attending Timothy Peat's Bible classes at Woodbrooke at this time, I was heartened to learn that the Greek which is translated as 'perfect' in the Authorised Version's 'be ye perfect as your father in heaven is perfect' (Matthew 5:48) can just as well be translated as 'whole'. Wholeness, rather than perfection, feels a much more realistic goal for a sinner like myself.

Gradually the elements of my journey were coming together. A greater degree of self-acceptance flowed from the self-knowledge of therapy, the re-membering of ritual and the humbling awareness of my capacity to fall short of my ideals. From the right perspective I could glimpse what Julian of Norwich meant by 'Sin is behovable [i.e. necessary or inevitable], but all shall be well, and all shall be well, and all manner of thing shall be well' (Julian of Norwich, 1966:35).

And then, suddenly, out of this period of darkness, new life was literally given to me. After ten years of our hoping for a child, Seren confirmed she was pregnant. The name we chose for our daughter – Hannah – means 'grace' or 'God has been gracious' and that was certainly how we both felt about this miraculous gift of life. From the depths of an experience of my own capacity to sin, the painful acceptance of who I am – no better and no worse – I came to appreciate atonement, at-one-ment, a sense of being restored to communion, to right relationship with God and others. Eight hours after she was born in our wardens' accommodation Hannah attended meeting for worship and two weeks later was accepted into membership. Her arrival confirmed our own sense of belonging among Friends while the seeds of my time at Woodbrooke continued to bear fruit.

8   Open to old light

It is not opinion, or speculation, or notions of what is true, or assent to or the subscription of articles or propositions, though never so soundly worded, that ... makes a man a true believer or a true Christian. But it is a conformity of mind and practice to the will of God, in all holiness of conversation, according to the dictates of this divine principle of Light and Life in the soul which denotes a person truly a child of God.
(William Penn, 1692, *QFP*, 26.78)

Through the crisis in my own life I was discovering what early Friends meant by 'turning to the Light' and how the Inward Light reveals us 'in our own particulars', as George Fox put it. I felt opened to a greater spiritual vulnerability, and I came to appreciate what Janey O'Shea meant when she said that in their writings early Friends used the word 'tender' in two ways – firstly as we use the adjective today to mean 'gentle' or 'sensitive' (as in 'being tender to one another') – but also as a verb much like the more recent 'tenderise', often in the passive voice in descriptions of being tendered by God through tribulation.

And in this difficult space, feeling very raw and vulnerable, I came to greatly value what early Friends spoke of as 'opportunities' or 'blessed opportunities'. I found there were times, as I was struggling to deal with the situation I was in, when I would be in conversation with a Friend and we just ran out of words, our minds and speech were stilled and we would fall into spontaneous prayerful silence. The deep sense of a quiet presence at such times was enormously refreshing both to my sleepless body and to the part of my mind that was still striving to be in control by *understanding* what had happened to me and why.

I was also hugely helped in this difficult time by being in a clearness committee formed to help me discern the lessons I needed to learn and what the way forward might be. In desperation I had finally learnt to ask for help. Three Friends met with me several times over a period of six months and held me in prayer as I gradually moved from denial through self-recrimination to humbling acceptance of my fallibility. This simple Quaker form – of a small group of people meeting to uphold the decision making of one amongst them – is one of the neglected pearls of our tradition (though more remembered in other yearly meetings) and has uses far beyond clearness for marriage.

In a clearness meeting questions are asked of the decision-maker out of the silence of worship, and the answers and insights that arise are written down for the focus person to reflect on afterwards. It is not a therapeutic process, though feelings may well up and flow freely. It is not a directive or advice-giving procedure, but time set aside in which those present prayerfully discern a deeper wisdom than that of the conscious, problem-solving mind. Truth is gently discovered rather than opinions or advice given. It is a living example of the 'quiet processes and small circles' to which Rufus Jones pinned his hopes (Vining, 1959:272). I felt so grateful for this support; I was astonished by the clarity that came from so simple a process as I felt the love and caring of these Friends. It helped to restore my faith when I was at my lowest ebb. It was another precious gift of Woodbrooke to have the time and space, as well as the experience of other Friends from yearly meetings around the world to draw on.

Whilst I learnt more about Quaker history and tradition, about controversies and schisms and about the diversity of Friends worldwide, I was still trying to make Quakerism fit the mould of my own preconceptions. I was secretly afraid of being further challenged in my beliefs and self-opinions, of having any more of my 'baggage' forcibly removed. Yet I had become a Friend because I was passionately committed to truth – even if that meant being open to the unexpected, even if it meant revisiting the Christianity of my childhood.

Having spent three terms at Woodbrooke as a student and having stayed on for two more terms as a Friend-in-Residence, I knew it was somewhere to which I would want to return repeatedly to tap the rich resources of people and facilities there. With the question asked of Damaris Parker-Rhodes still gnawing away at me, I enrolled in 1997 for Timothy Peat's short course on 'Quakers and Christ'. I went to open myself further to what we meant by 'the Christian roots of Quakerism'. But try as I might I could not get beyond the sense deep within me that the story of Jesus is a religious *myth*, in the true sense of the term – 'not', as John Polkinghorne points out, 'a falsehood but a truth conveyed in narrative form, because only story could carry the necessary depth of meaning.' (Polkinghorne, 1998:64). And I found myself once more reacting against the way that Christianity has, as Joseph Campbell put it, 'literalised the myth' (Campbell, 1989).

As anyone who has been there knows, education at Woodbrooke is never solely a matter of the mind; the whole person is involved and learning is as likely to happen over coffee as in the library or teaching sessions. The delight of honest dialogue, of mutual vulnerability, of personal discovery and shared illumination is excitingly infectious. Other short courses I attended also led me into a deeper understanding of Quaker-Christianity. There were several occasions in Marion McNaughton's courses on Jewish-Christian relations when I was moved to tears – both at the injustice and prejudice that Jews have suffered but also because hearing Hebrew prayers spoken or sung stirred a deep 'memory' of long-forgotten, meaningful religious ritual and observance – as if my heritage was vaster, richer, more ancient than anything I had been taught. As I heard Jewish people speaking of their faith, I felt a profound sense of healing, of finding the missing pieces, of making whole.

From my studies and encounters at Woodbrooke I came away willing to acknowledge the historical, human Jesus as a teacher and example, but finding it not merely intellectually impossible but, surprisingly, actually *offensive* to accord him the supernatural status of 'Christ'. Unlike early Friends, we have now been exposed to a wealth of biblical scholarship and archaeological evidence which casts light on the origins of Christianity. We can now imaginatively enter the Jewish world of two thousand years ago probably more fully than any previous generation. And when I did this in study or prayer, when I opened myself to that encounter, what I came to was a sense of the radical faithfulness of a man who gave himself utterly to the power of his God. But I also found myself strongly aligned with the Jewish 'No' to Jesus as the Messiah. I identify with their sense of blasphemous outrage at the claims of Paul and his followers, at the idolatry of worshipping Jesus *as* God.

For in Jesus I find a model of sacrificial faithfulness to the guidance of the Spirit, of utter transparency to the divine – even though I still have great difficulty approaching the Bible because of childhood violation. Certainly his story speaks of God suffering intimately in the world with us, but for me the poignancy of that revelation does not depend on a belief that God uniquely entered history two thousand years ago (not least because of the way it has been portrayed as the 'supersession' of the faithfulness and testimony of the Jewish people). I cannot accept that the Creator has ever been absent from the creation or that the world in general has ever 'fallen' or been in need of redemption.

Asked now 'in what sense I would call myself a Christian', I have to answer that I now describe myself as a 'post-christian'.

I am certainly not post-anything-else; it is the Christian tradition which has formed the culture I live in and which has profoundly, if erratically, influenced the orientation of my head and heart. To a person of any other faith I am obviously and profoundly *culturally* a Christian – whatever I profess to believe. But 'Christian' has come to mean someone who accepts certain *beliefs about* Jesus. Asked point-blank if I believe him to be the unique and final revelation of God, the second aspect of a divine Trinity, the saviour of the world, who offered himself on the cross to atone for all human sin and who rose from the dead into heaven, where he sits at God's right hand to judge the living and the dead – I would have to say that in the Quaker experience these are the wrong questions! In an important sense I feel in exile, neither wholeheartedly part of, yet not clearly separate from, the religious heritage of my country and my ancestors.

But in the accounts of Friends' lives and witness I was touched by something in the metaphoric language they used, something deeper than the words we use to define ourselves, something that enabled me to keep struggling with the tradition rather than merely dismiss it outright.

One of the ways I enjoy using the Woodbrooke library is to browse the shelves and see what 'jumps out at me'. In this serendipitous way I have found many gems, which often spoke deeply to my condition at that particular moment. One day I came across Margaret Hope Bacon's account of how Lucretia Mott was censured by her elders for giving this ministry: '[Men] are to be judged by their likeness to Christ, rather than their notions of Christ' – until Mott pointed out that the words were those of William Penn (Bacon, 1980:37).

This resonated with me, for I recognised now – in my own small way – what early Friends spoke of as the experience of the Cross. What was opening to me was an appreciation of Quakerism as a path of faithful *surrender*. The essence of Quaker spirituality – which placed it squarely within the Christian tradition but also distinguished it in a way I didn't yet fully understand – was the individual and collective mystical experience of the guiding presence of an intensely personal sense of God. Its hallmark was the surrendered life, the giving over of oneself to that God, at whatever personal cost. This was not about self-sacrifice of a morbid kind but pointed to a ministry of total vulnerability, a relinquishing of control and personal ambition, which might include a willingness to suffer.

At this point of intense openness in my own life, I began to understand things I had been reading in a new light. At about this time I was introduced to Stephen Crisp's moving account of the ministry and last days of James Parnell's brief life:

> After he had passed up and down many parts of that county [Essex], and planted diverse good Meetings, and confirmed them that had believed; he at length ... came to Colchester ... and ... preached the Gospel unto many thousands of people ... and after that disputed with the Town Lecturer and another priest in the French School, all in one day: in all which the Wisdom, Power and Patience of Christ appeared very gloriously, to the convincing of my self and many more, who were witnesses of that day's work: ... many did believe ... and others were hardened, and rebelled against the Appearance of Truth, and became enemies, with whom he disputed daily in great soundness, ... by which also many were reached, and convinced of the Truth, and the mouths of gainsayers stopped; which made many gnash their teeth on him; and some undertook to club out the priests and professors arguments by beating this dear lamb with fists and staves, who took all patiently; ... one who struck him with a great staff as he came out of one of the steeplehouses ... said 'There, take that, for Jesus Christ's sake'; to which he returned this answer 'Friend, I do receive it for Jesus Christ's sake'. And many other intolerable affronts were offered him, in all which his Spirit was not seen to be raised in heat or

anger, but was a pattern of patience and meekness. And having laboured in that great town about ten days, it lay upon him to go back to Cogshall ... from when he was committed to Colchester Castle, and from there up to Chelmsford Assizes in irons, and again thither re-committed, where he remained until he offered up his life for his testimony. (Crisp, 1675)

This account of a calling to faithful vulnerability, together with my own experience of being tendered, took me beyond my intellectual difficulties with Christianity into a sense of humility in the face of mystery. Yet at the same time it took me into the heart of what seemed to *distinguish* Quakers from other Christians, our reclaiming of 'Christ' from the dogmas of the Church. When in the nineteenth century Elias Hicks affirmed that 'the anointing spirit of God is within you', he was arguing that 'Christ' was not of flesh and blood:

It was that life, that same life ... that was in him [Jesus], and which is the light and life of men, and which lights every man, and consequently every woman, that comes into the world. And we have this light and life in us; which is what the apostle meant by Jesus Christ; and if we have not this ruling in us then we are dead, because we are not under the law of the spirit of life. (Elias Hicks, 1827, in Abbott, 1997:215-6)

I felt I was finally beginning to square the circle, to bring what I had experienced in diverse other places and forms – experiences of the Spirit in spontaneous rituals, in seasonal circles, in being real with one another and in simple acts of human kindness – with the faith and practice of the Quaker-Christian community I had felt led amongst.

For Hicks was pointing to an experience central to Quaker faith; not a *belief in* something external but an inner knowing; Truth not as a concept, an idea or a doctrine but as a reality we can and must experience within ourselves. I finally realised why early Friends stressed this quality of 'experimental' knowing – which makes them seem so extremely modern

> Not that thou shouldst believe upon my authority, nothing less – for that's not to act on knowledge but trust – but thou shouldst try and approve what I write, for that is all I ask, as well as I need, for thy conviction and my own justification. The whole being but a spiritual experiment upon the soul, and therefore seeks no implicit credit, because it is self-evident to them that will uprightly try it. (Penn, 1993:228)

My attention was drawn to this passage by Rex Ambler, who was to further the reconciliation of my twentieth-century experiences with my understanding of Quaker tradition. Rex had spent over two years studying the writings of early Friends researching the fundamental *experience* that gave them their distinctive identity, that distinguished them from credal Christian denominations. He was excited to discover a clear step-by-step process, spoken of in many different metaphors but to which Rex gave the title 'Experiment with Light'.

Early Friends, of course, never spelt out the process in this way. Ironically, this process could not be 'outwardly preached' for its aim was 'the end of all words' and outward forms of religion. George Fox only devised it after despairing of other sources of revelation, only when he turned from the 'separate' [independent] preachers and 'the most experienced people' and heard the voice *within himself* that told him 'there was one, even Christ Jesus who could speak to his condition' (i.e. show him his brokenness, his separation from God, all the things he might wish to deny or disown) (QFP, 19.02).

Rex identified the following steps (quotations from George Fox unless otherwise stated):

Look inside: 'Your teacher is within you; look not forth'. *Identify the light*: 'there is something riseth in you that is a witness against you, and that is the Light'. *Let the light show you yourself*: 'As the Light opens and exercises thy conscience, it will ... let thee see invisible things'. *Trace the light to its source*: 'Ye query, What God really is in himself? ... My counsel to you is, to stand still in his own counsel, namely his Light in your own consciences, that in that you may be led forth into his life and likeness' (Samuel Fisher). *Trust the light to show you the alternative*: 'For looking down at sin, and corruption, and distraction, you are swallowed up in it; but looking at the light that discovers them, you will see over them'. *Feel the new life grow*: 'So the Light shineth forth in the Darkness, to visit the Seed shut up therein, and the Light breathes Life into the Seed' (George Keith). *See other people in the light*: 'Abiding inwardly in the Light, it will let you see one another and the unity one with another'. *See the world in the light*: 'This Light, which is of God, lets thee see all the works of the world, and draws thee out of the worships of the world, and keeps thee in the fear of God'. *Learn to love in the light*: "Here is gospel for thee, here is my hair and here is my cheeks and here are my shoulders", and turned them to him ... and the Truth came so over him that he grew loving.' (Ambler, 1997 – all sources given there)

Rex's researches revealed Friends using this process of turning to the Light on three distinct levels – as individuals (stilling oneself and listening within), in community (nurturing and encouraging one another to 'dwell' in the Light, as each has only 'a measure' of the Light) and, finally, engaging with the world, 'answering' (awakening/eliciting) the light within others. Creating a form of meditation based on this spiritual process, Rex found it had strong parallels with a modern therapeutic practice called Focusing.

I first experienced the workshop process Rex subsequently devised during a Quaker Retreat Group week at Charney Manor. I felt I was being led into the heart of Quaker spirituality. The process began with an invitation to *relax body and mind*, to get comfortable and put aside the thoughts and expectations that usually preoccupy our waking hours. Becoming wholly receptive, we were invited to *let the real concerns of our life emerge*, in particular, to notice anything we might be feeling uncomfortable or uneasy about. In stillness, beyond conscious control, we were then asked to *focus on one issue or relationship* that was troubling us. Without thinking about it or being distracted by what we might feel, we were told to *let the Light show us what is really happening*, what this is really about. In the silence an image might come or a single word, or perhaps a general feeling sense or an awareness in the body. All the time we were invited to stay receptive and merely keep gently asking *why is it like that*, and, waiting in the Light, allow an answer to come, and then wait until further clarity might arise within us. As we started to emerge from the meditation we were encouraged to *welcome the answer that came*, however unexpected, trusting the Light and submitting to its guidance.

As each person in the group quietly accepted the truth revealed in this way there was for many a deep sense of peace, of relief; for others a muted sadness or a not-so-quiet sense of sheer joy. Those who felt nothing much had happened were invited to try again when it might feel safer or otherwise more appropriate. This was a process that we would benefit from going through again and again. As we completed the meditation people then spent time alone reflecting, journalling or walking in the grounds before sharing what they had experienced in small groups later in the day. It may not sound much described in this way, but Friends found it a powerful, illuminating process, a valuable 'reframing' of early Friends' experience, not a substitute for meeting for worship but a helpful complement to it.

Here was what I had been looking for since joining Friends. This experiential work helped me to make sense of how Quakerism is both rooted in Christian tradition and yet able to speak in such universal terms. Now I understood how early Friends could have believed themselves the only true Christians – the ones who would bring the Church out of its 'apostasy' and back to its true foundations – while deliberately speaking in metaphors (of the Light, or Seed, or Guide within) which avoided dogmatic formulations of exactly what this 'something' of God within us was.

This distinctive Quaker emphasis meant that Friends did not (like the Puritans around them) believe in the salvation of an Elect but were inclusive in a truly radical way – not in the modern sense of 'anything goes' but in a profound sense of trusting that this inner guidance was available to all who followed the discipline of submitting to its leadings. As Francis Howgill expressed it:

> Why may not the Heathen have the Light of the Spirit? ... The grace of God hath appeared unto all men. And who art thou that makes exceptions? Though the Heathen do not know Christ of the Spirit by the name of Christ and Spirit, ... they have the thing ... and I say, Nay, these men were not born without Light ... God is rich unto all. (Edwards, 1992:26)

I began to understand how the writings of early Friends could seem so inaccessible because they are so steeped in archaic 'Christian' language and yet how early Quakers could be condemned by their contemporaries as not even Christians! At a deep place, the place 'beyond words', it was not important what we called ourselves – which is why the experience of silent meeting can be so powerful. What matters is the commitment to and the quality of our surrendering.

As I struggled to reconcile the apparent contradictions of a Quaker-Christian identity, Seren one day offered me the image of a stained-glass window: the Light itself comes from one Source, though it shines through the many coloured images of divinity we create. Early Friends, in pointing us beyond the window towards the Source of illumination itself, did so in the only imagery and language available to them: that of the window of the Christian story. But in using words and images drawn from Christianity they were also aware that these were human notions, which distract us from what is really important. The glass, however beautiful and however attached we may personally be to a particular set of panes, is but a one-dimensional surface, whose purpose is to allow the light to pass through. What matters is not the religious imagery that has meaning for us but the act of turning to the Light that is both beyond the window and deep within us all.

One of the most powerful aspects of working with the 'Experiment with Light' was the experience of knowing in a group when we were hearing truth. This tallied exactly with my own experiences of authentic ritual and of ministry in a truly gathered meeting. There was a quality of depth to it, an authority that simply could not be argued with (that 'stopped the mouths of gainsayers'). And what was extraordinary (to me as a modern individual) was that in seeking truth in this way, the truth that was discovered was not an individual thing. Truth revealed in this way is not 'my truth', which, once sensed within me I must assert against or above the truth others discover within; the truth I connect with when I truly surrender will lead me, if I am obedient to it, into unity with others – an experience central to Quakers from the earliest times. It is as if, like fragments of a hologram, we are all aspects of one whole and in the stillness of what we call Quaker worship we can get beneath our ego separations and be reminded of this greater pattern, whatever name we give to it. To live in the Light is to be open to this awareness and seek to be obedient to its guidance at all times.

From working with this process, I learnt that when I am supported (and challenged) to live in this more open way, I do not need to turn to others to be told what to do, I do not need to inhibit my deepest convictions, nor need I cling to structures – whether schedules or codified principles of behaviour – to guide me; the whole of my life becomes an experiment in obedience and discernment. Truth is then neither a philosophical notion nor a matter of ethical principles – even ones as worthy as the Quaker testimonies. Such codifying of behaviour is actually *the very opposite* of the experience to which Quakerism points us, which is obedience to something alive and dependable within, a source of revelation available to all beyond any system of religious belief. This is surely what Penn meant by the 'one religion' of the humble, just and meek (*QFP*, 19.28) – this was not prescriptive, how we *should* live, but descriptive, how we will live when we are 'dwelling in the light'.

When, today, we find ourselves not in unity, perhaps it is because we have not really reached this place of surrender in ourselves on which the Quaker process depends. This place 'beyond words' is also potentially a meeting point with other denominations and faiths. For whilst Quakerism clearly arose within the Protestant Reformation of the Christian Church (there was no way early Friends could have framed their experience in any other terms) what it became was not merely another set of sectarian notions or structures: it emerged as a potentially universal practice that reveals truth as the reality beyond our self-images and deceptions.

What the process of Quaker spiritual discipline offers is a way of discerning the Reality that is waiting to emerge when we can get beyond our egocentricity and participate in the 'becomingness' of God. All the images early Friends used of 'the Tempter', 'the Deceiver' and the 'creaturely' point to the many attachments we have that obscure this underlying Reality, the many ways we have of ignoring or obstructing the 'promptings of love and truth in our hearts'. In an epistle to Friends written in 1652, George Fox understood the power of our attachments and the persistence needed to confront them only too well:

Whatever ye are addicted to, the Tempter will come in that thing: and when he can trouble you, then he gets advantage over you, and then ye are gone. Stand still in that which is pure, after ye see yourselves; and then mercy comes in. After thou sees thy thoughts, and the temptation, do not think, but submit, and then power comes. Stand still in that which it shows and discovers, and there doth strength immediately come. And stand still in the Light, and submit to it, and the other will be hushed and gone; and then content comes. And when temptations and troubles appear, sink down in that which is pure, and all will be hushed and fly away. ... If ye do anything in your own wills, then ye tempt God; but stand still in the Power, which brings peace.
(Fox, 1698:11)

9 Learning to pray anew

I agree there is a power, a mystery, a vast force beyond
human comprehension, but I don't see that power as
outside us or as a male figure. My image is a cooperative
union between the power of the Universe and my own
will. I ask the Universe to energise my will. Instead of
praying to God to take care of me, I ask for the
strength to take action. And I believe we can find that
power through prayer, meditation, affirmations,
exercise, being with people, going to talks and
workshops and simply opening our senses to all that is
around us because God/the Goddess, or the power of
the Universe, is everywhere, in all living things. It's not
'out there'. Likewise there is a mystery involved in the
process, because while we can take action, ultimately
we can't tell a gift how to come. The form of the
outcome is still out of our hands to some degree, but
we can help guide the course. (Kasl, 1992:311)

A few months ago I visited Wells Cathedral shortly before it
closed for the night. As the building was being locked up I
found my way through the cloisters to a side door that brought
me into the transept, right by the votive candles lit by other
visitors. As I looked up into the vast body of the building I
found myself moved to tears at the awesomeness of the

Nameless One to whose glory such a structure was created. I added another candle and said a silent prayer. Walking round the emptying building I entered one of the small side chapels and knelt there to pray, something I rarely do in a meeting house.

I find myself visiting 'steeple houses' not for their services but for the sense of continuity, of faithful obedience to the unspeakable majesty of God which they were built to honour. For as a late twentieth-century Friend I have great difficulty in encountering this sense of God as wholly Other in meeting for worship. The God of the Quakers often seems too small, reduced to the familiar and comfortable 'that of God within'. Personally, if I can claim to have encountered the God of the Bible, it would be in wild places, on open hillsides and wind-swept moors. There I meet a God I can shout at and rail against, and whose winds knock me to the ground as we argue in a thoroughly 'unQuakerly' way. My sense is that God can take it.

I arrived at Wells Cathedral after one of my sessions with a healer and body-worker near Glastonbury, who works surrounded by Goddess figurines and a sculpture of Ganesh, the Hindu elephant deity, whose healing space smells of woodsmoke and incense and from whose ceiling hangs a Native American 'dream-catcher'. Not only am I happy to inhabit these two very different spiritual cultures but I know, deep within me, that I *have* to span them. Without the creative, holistic experimentation of what is called 'the New Age', without its energy, playfulness and radicalism, its marriage of head and heart, of science and mysticism, I would reject outright the stultifying irrelevance of what I learnt as religion in my childhood. And without the living tradition and continuity that Christianity at its best represents, the 'New Age' would seem hopelessly naïve, lacking in discipline or focus.

When I think of my closest friends, none of them (outside Quaker circles) relate their spiritual journeys to either the Christian Church or the Bible in any conscious way, though they are all sincere spiritual seekers. If I were to characterise (and inevitably caricature) their spiritual paths, they would include a Zen Buddhist, a one-time devotee of Bhagwan who also meditates, a practitioner and teacher of Native American medicine wheel, a couple of 'lapsed' Catholics, a story-telling Celt who practises yoga daily, various kinds of earth-centred pagans, and several more who, for want of any other designation, might be termed 'New Agers'.

This variety reflects how we are now living 'between stories', in a time when the hegemony, the spiritual monopoly of the Christian Church in this country has passed and when church religion is irrelevant to a growing majority of the population. Christianity, though still claiming special status in our education system and in public ceremonial life, is conceding ground all the time to those of other faiths and those who are 'unchurched'. With a diversity of spiritual paths available to us, there is a danger of a 'pick 'n' mix' attitude to religion (in which we avoid the discipline of staying with one path long enough for it to illuminate the dark corners of our being) or of spirituality becoming a matter of privatised 'consumer choice', a commodity to be packaged and sold as books, tapes, and workshops. But the spiritual hunger evident in people's searching is real enough and something we are called to acknowledge and 'answer' as Friends.

In this 'post-christian' age the Christian story can no longer presume to be the sole explanatory myth underpinning cultural life. In a multi-faith, multi-cultural society, in the light of all we know of human spiritual and religious diversity, its claim to be *the* universalising story of humankind is unsustainable. And from a postmodern perspective the ideal of a single, grand unifying model or system is untenable anyway. The study of comparative religion reveals that there is no such thing as a pure tradition; religions evolve and 'irradiate' each other over time and between cultures. In fact, evolutionary theory and comparative studies of religion have – together with biblical scholarship – played a significant part in undermining the pre-eminence of Christianity over the last hundred years.

Whatever the reason, large numbers of people today – both

inside and outside the Church – are searching for a creative kind of spirituality, one that affirms passion, expressiveness, creativity, diversity, mindfulness and joy. They are searching for a life-loving spirituality, one that reminds us that we are born blessed and holy and in which the goal of our lives is to grow, to expand and to feel connected to all life. What is emerging is the call for a faith that does not set itself against rationality or the findings of science. For science, as it probes and now learns to participate in the universe, can actually enhance our awareness of awe and wonder. When astronaut Michael Collins first looked out at our planet from space, his poetic description was filled with a sense of mystery:

> The more we see of other planets, the better this one looks. When I travelled to the Moon it wasn't just my proximity to that battered rock pile I remember so vividly, but rather what I saw when I looked back at my fragile home, a glistening, inviting beacon, delicate blue and white, a tiny outpost suspended in the black infinity. Earth is to be treasured and nurtured, something precious that must endure. (Rolston, 1996:408)

As Jung predicted, the sight of our planet from space has had a profound impact on our collective consciousness. We can all now visualise our planet as literally a finite sphere of awesome mystery, the location of a complex unfolding of diverse natural and cultural histories, a place of untold richness, both precious and fragile against the dark void of space. The more we are aware of it, the more the story of life on earth appears to be a series of 'miracles', of wondrous and fortuitous events, the unfolding of a mysterious potential, an awesome mixture of 'accident' and necessity. Thomas Berry sees this awareness calling forth a new spirituality, one which 'emerges out of a reality deeper than ourselves, even deeper than life, a spirituality that is as deep as the earth process itself, a spirituality born out of the solar system and even out of the heavens beyond the solar system' (Berry, 1990:155).

Our current questioning of our identity as Friends needs to be seen in the context of this emerging new sense of who we are and the universe we inhabit, of the cultural 'paradigm shift' which will affect all aspects of both secular and religious life. Theologian and liturgist Jim Cotter describes our times as characterised by a shift:

> from the logical and rational to the intuitive and affective; from thinking of human beings as souls encased in flesh to appreciating that we are whole persons living as bodies; from truth in timeless propositions, handed down complete from one generation to the next, to truth as revealed in the dialogue between our own story and the stories we have inherited; from structures and forms to processes and relationships; from building blocks to networks of links and nodes which glow and fade; ... from an analysis of individual atoms to a symphony of persons in community; from separation and isolation to connection and diversity. (Cotter, 1993:6)

What have Quakers to contribute to this new awareness? In *The World in my Heart*, Jo Farrow points out that George Fox justified Quaker worship on the basis of a conversation that Jesus had 'about the end of formal religion and the beginning of a new age of the Spirit in which real prayer and worship will be understood in terms of what really goes on inside people at the deepest places in their lives, "in spirit and in truth"'. She continues:

> It is not religion that matters so much. It is life. It is not religion that requires our deepest respect and reverence. It is life. The life springing up in ourselves and others, the life of all living things and of the planet on which we pursue our inter-connected lives. (Farrow, 1990:119)

We often now define our Quaker faith by our testimonies or by our vague new proto-creed of 'that of God in everyone'. Quakers wisely avoid theology in the sense of speculation about the Unspeakable, but if we are to be true to our heritage and 'answer' the many seekers of our time we need to clarify and articulate our experience of truth, of the guidance of what we call God, in imagery appropriate to this new age of the spirit – an age which Jesus heralded and to which early Friends believed they had returned.

If humankind is evolving slowly but surely beyond a sense of God as 'external, supernatural, and invasive', an omnipotent parent-figure (which as Freud suggested, humanity created to reassure itself), then we need to ask, with James Spong, the bishop of Newark, not *who* God is but *what* God is. He cites one possibility as the ancient Hebrew concept of God as *ruach* or wind, observed not as a being but as 'a vitalizing force' (Spong, 1998:54).

In this postmodern age, when the language of probability is replacing even the certainties of science, perhaps, like the Jewish people of old in exile, we are having to learn to sing a new song in a strange land:

> There is no God external to life. God, rather, is the inescapable depth and centre of all that is. God is not a being superior to all other beings. God is the ground of being itself ... The artifacts of the faith of the past must be understood in a new way if they are to accompany us beyond the exile, and those that cannot be understood differently will have to be laid aside. (Spong, 1998:70)

If, as Spong suggests, we conceptualise our God as 'a presence that we call "transcendent" and "beyond" and that yet is never apart from who we are or what the world is ... a presence in the heart of our life that could never be invoked as a being but nonetheless might be entered as a divine and infinite reality', our faith then becomes a matter of opening ourselves to such a reality, becoming intensely aware of it, and having 'both our being and our consciousness expanded by it' (Spong, 1998:60). In opening ourselves in this way, we may be helped as much by our poets as by our theologians:

> 'God is subtle,' Einstein said, 'but not malicious. ... nature conceals her mystery by means of her essential grandeur, not by her cunning' ... It could be that God has not absconded but spread, as our vision and understanding of the universe have spread, to a fabric of spirit and sense so grand and subtle, so powerful in a new way, that we can only feel blindly of its hem. (Dillard, 1995:286)

Perhaps, in this 'between times', this explains why there is less vocal prayer in meeting for worship than there used to be. The old ways of talking to God simply do not work for many of us. The sense of prayer as petitioning a distant, omnipotent Ruler of the Universe, a divine rescuer who will sort out our human messes, is appealing but untenable. And yet I know I feel a yearning for a life of prayer, a sense of conversational communion with the Source of all being. It is one of the things that differentiates worship from meditation.

So I have to find a way of praying that my mind can accept, that doesn't seem superstitious; I have to find a way, as Abbot John Chapman put it, to 'pray as I can, not as I can't'. Prayer needs to include the whole of who I am – body, mind, spirit, temperament. If my sense of God is as the vitalising presence within creation, within the world, within each one of us, this points to a new kind of prayer. Prayer becomes a matter of stilling my busyness and self-preoccupation, opening my awareness to what *is*, becoming attentive and receptive to what might be, to that which is trying to be born. Prayer then is an activity with no observable action, an aligning of my small self with the 'heart and mind' of the Universe.

I sense a difficulty here for us as Friends: we have made such a virtue of being 'in the world' that many of us have become caught up in what Thomas Merton called the 'real sickness' of feeling we have to keep moving, always inordinately active, treating time as a commodity like the rest of secular society (de Waal, 1992:40). It's as if we have forgotten that engagement requires withdrawal, as if we no longer value the time-honoured practice of religious retreat. I know some of my most lasting experiences of the Spirit have occurred either in nature or in the company of others who have temporarily withdrawn from the demands of our overbusy modern world. The American Quaker Jim Corbett addresses just how hard it is for us as late twentieth-century Friends simply to *be*:

> To learn why you feel compelled to remake and consume the world, live alone in wilderness for at least a week. Take no books or other distractions. Take simple, adequate food that requires little or no preparation. Don't plan things to do when the week is over. Don't do yoga or meditation that you think will result in self-improvement. Simply do nothing ... Just cease to intervene and plan. Do nothing but celebrate the goodness of creation – if you can ... Here's what you may learn: The most attractive surroundings removed from consumption and busyness will be a hell for you. To discover the uses of uselessness you must be reborn into the present. (Corbett, 1991:5)

Being 'reborn into the present' is an essential part of Friends' 'earthy mysticism' for me. As mystics we bear witness to the miraculous presence, the unnamable mystery at the very heart of life. I remember a time at the end of one of the week-long men's events in the mountains of north Wales. After six days of sharing together, of singing and crying, laughing and drumming, of dancing and spending time silently in nature, I woke on the last morning of the group just before sunrise.

Reviving the embers of the previous night's fire, waiting for the billy-can to boil, I watched the sun rise slowly over the valley in front of me as a heron suddenly rose from beside the lake and with laborious slow beats of its wings made its way over my head and off down the valley.

In that perfect moment I felt exhausted and totally, magnificently, gratefully alive. In my tiredness I was vulnerable to the miracle of the dawning day, my senses were heightened, my body felt cleansed by what we had shared and I saw and smelt the world around me as if for the first time. I *remembered* who I really was as I sat there enjoying a gloriously inhabited solitude. In human terms I was alone but this for me was a profoundly *religious* moment, a time when I had the experience of being taken out of my small sense of self and tied back into a greater reality. It was a grace, totally unwilled and unexpected, when I was reminded of the mysterious covenant of life, of laws more ancient and binding than anything written in a book or devised by the human mind. In that moment I simply felt myself *a part of*, not *apart from*, the commonwealth of life.

As our sense of God changes, so too will our practice of prayer and worship. When I feel myself fully absorbed in an activity, when I allow my life to be adjusted by an intuitive sense of what is appropriate in that moment, when I am grateful, when I consciously choose to participate in the creative unfolding of the universe – remembering that each of us is a unique manifestation of a four-and-a-half-billion-year evolutionary process – all these, I now accept, are moments of prayer.

10 Stand still – and dance!

The modern age was characterised by isolation and
loneliness, but the postmodern age will rediscover the
power of community and kinship with all beings ... Base
communities, more than ecclesiastical bureaucracies,
hold the future to spirituality. (Fox, 1996:279)

If I can't dance to it, it's not my revolution.
(attributed to Emma Goldman)

I was present recently at two extremely powerful meetings for
worship. The first was a memorial meeting held for a woman
who had been to our meeting only once but whose adult
children felt instinctively that our meeting house was the right
place to remember her. In a packed meeting room, people
spoke out of the silence, movingly invoking the mother, wife
and colleague they had known. One of her sons played his
guitar and sang a song much loved by the family; others offered
tributes of poems or heartfelt spontaneous words of gratitude
for her life. Some ministries were eloquent and articulate,
others were fumbling, rough and raw. Tears flowed freely and
laughter filled the room. All of us present were moved, and
although I had never met her, her presence was palpable in the
room that afternoon. The few Quakers present, attending to
ensure all was 'in right ordering', felt we were given a precious

gift that day – the experience of an uninhibited, powerful, spontaneous expression of the Spirit of God moving in the hearts of ordinary women and men, a beautiful example of a Quaker meeting.

When the hour was up, the elders present sensed there was much life in this meeting still and we 'allowed' the meeting to continue for another twenty minutes. Even as we shook hands and ended the meeting for the sake of those who had to leave to meet the pressing demands of their lives, we knew that this meeting could have ebbed and peaked and quietly flowed on for a good while longer.

Another vivid memory I have is of a Quaker men's weekend at Swarthmoor Hall. After a day and a half of sharing deeply together, walking by the Lakes and lighting an evening bonfire on the beach, on the Sunday morning we began with movement and stretching in the cold autumnal air. Then one man led us in several rounds of singing before, making the most of our last morning in the Lakes together, we piled into two cars for one last walk in the hills. After a short, brisk climb we reached a small inviting tarn, where some of us swam. Returning to the hall we centred down together into a most profound stillness, a deeply nourishing sense of Presence. I can't recall a time before or since when I came to meeting with heart and mind *and body* so well prepared.

My vision for the future is of our Quaker meetings coming alive as base communities of a new postmodern, post-denominational spirituality rooted in the distinctive Quaker form of Christian witness and so answering the spiritual awakening of our age. Friends are so well placed to play a part in this! We could be radical, evolutionary cells where the discipline of opening to the Inner Light is taught and each person's journey is honoured as part of an emerging process of truth-telling and discovery. Groups of different sizes could meet to worship, to celebrate together, to challenge and support each other to listen to the inner guide and so to live more faithful lives. Meeting houses could be places where we combine these spiritual practices with community-based activities – talks and support-groups for simple living, explorations of our 'deep' ecology, actions for peace and justice-making. Without the burdens of dogmas, liturgy and a separate priesthood, we are potentially free to experiment with our worship, to explore what is in our hearts, to put Penn's 'experiment in the human soul' to the test. It could be as simple a matter as moving the benches – or their equivalent.

I remember, at Woodbrooke, Janey O'Shea speaking of three criteria for the renewal of any religious movement: the first was an understanding of the founding charism and particular vocation of the group; the second was an accurate reading of 'the signs of the times'; and finally, perhaps most importantly, was a personal willingness to be renewed (see O'Shea, 1993:60-65). Is fear of this what most inhibits us? Margaret Fell promised that 'the light will rip you open'; Quaker spirituality has never been a soft option. Yet it has so much to offer the world today when the kind of faith we are being called to is one of increasing vulnerability and receptivity, an openness to Reality and to who we really are, to the truth revealed in our hearts moment by moment.

The challenge of our times is to build bridges of all kinds. As Marcus Braybrooke, former director of the Council for Christians and Jews helpfully points out: 'Faith ... involves a constant search for a deeper awareness of the Divine Mystery, not a holding on to fixed doctrines. In that search today, if we will, we may be illuminated by the insights of all the great spiritual traditions' (Braybrooke, 1990:1).

Perhaps in this time of upheaval, of mourning for old certainties, of uncertainty about the future on so many levels, it helps to remember that faith is a verb, something that grows and changes with age and experience. Faith is a journey that has different stages, with times of great leaps and periods of inevitable aridity. We need to be tender with one another, helping each other face our fears and engaging in dialogue from our different faith 'stages' and in our diverse religious dialects.

Doug Gwyn speaks of his own 'bispirituality', of his moving in the realms of both evangelical and liberal Friends: 'covenant faithfulness requires that we learn to respect and welcome the sensibility that is alien to us' (Gwyn, 1996:78). He believes that:

> Today, God wills to work through the dialogue and cooperation between many peoples of many faiths and nonfaiths, and between people following different paths of faithful love. I believe this, and I see it happening in many seemingly unrelated experiments around us. (Gwyn, 1996:79)

I see the potential for Quakers to be a holistic learning (disciple) community, and for our meeting houses to be exciting venues catering to body, mind and spirit, meeting the challenge John MacMurray posed us: to become a real community in the world, not for our own sake but for the sake of the world (MacMurray, 1965). I see us as a community of all ages that grows together through worship, learning and play, through projects for making justice and peace, a community that really knows how to *enjoy* itself, that uses our wonderful resources of people and places, of serious discernment and creative foolishness, to reinvent religion itself.

I want us to echo the words of Chung Hyun Kyung: 'Let us welcome the Spirit, letting ourselves go in her wild rhythm of life', trusting our heart-memory, the cellular intelligence that has brought us through four and a half billion years of evolution to this moment in time. I pray for us to be passionate and unpredictable as well as prudent (which we do so well), unfettered by convention or precedent, but informed by experience, always alive to the Spirit in all, soul-full, expressive, compassionate and seeking wisdom and the truth revealed to us in the moment, respecting the God-given gift of the sensuous, understanding the erotic as life's longing for communion with itself.

I long for us to promote a cosmological sense of religion, bringing together science, mysticism and the creative arts in experimental worship, in new forms of celebration and lamentation needed in these exciting and threatening times, arising from expectant waiting and what Patricia Loring calls a 'listening spirituality' (Loring, 1997). I would love *all* of us to be leaven in this way rather than project this role onto the Leaveners or Young Friends (no matter how splendidly both groups embody that vitality).

I want to encourage every one of us to have a vision of who we are and why we are Friends, spoken of in the language that has meaning for us, a vision that inspires us (and therefore those around us), that breathes *life* into our desire for justice and peace for the whole of creation. (I do not want to be a dutiful Quaker.) I want us to revive our evangelical spirit – not in the imitation of early Friends but because we have our own Good News to share and cannot help conversing with others about what we have found. Enthusiasm means 'God within' and that, in a quite specific sense, is such an important part of our Quaker gospel!

I see us as bridge people, assisting the traffic between the traditional and the being-born, rooted in both mysticism – the immediate *experience* of divinity nurtured by both engagement with and retreat or withdrawal from 'the world' – and prophecy – *involvement with* and action on behalf of the oppressed, the forgotten, the used and abused, the voiceless of the earth. But as we work in exciting, creative ways for peace and justice we must not forget our own needs and limitations, indeed our sinfulness, if we can reclaim the word.

Let us avoid the sense of duty and sacrifice that taints those who *do good to* others. As Australian aborigine Lila Watson expresses it so forcefully: 'If you have come to help me – you are wasting your time; but if you have come because your liberation is bound up in mine – then let us work together.'

I see us as a paradoxically joyous and penitential community, whose business is quite simply the redemption of the world.

For some of us personal healing, dealing with our own pain, is an overwhelming priority; others will be called to live out their witness on the world's stage. All are needed; every one of us has a part to play in what Rosemary Radford Ruether calls 'the *kindom* of God'.

As someone who tends to seriousness myself, I am inspired by the words of Rebbe Nachman of Breslov: 'Always remember: Joy is not merely incidental to your spiritual quest. It is vital' (Mykoff, 1994:99). I sense a great flowering, a tremendous release of potential, of imagination and creativity as Quakers 'join the dance' of those many souls committed to finding a new way of being human on this planet, a different consciousness for men and women.

My vision is of a passionate, juicy Quakerism, of disciplined rebels and surrendered individualists, a creative order of mundane religious, a company of mutually encouraging, authentic and inspiring fools for that God who is the Source of everything. Honouring both our specific radical Christian witness and the universal nature of the Light Within, perhaps we can make our small, significant Quaker contribution to the emerging new awareness and, ultimately, to the survival of life on earth.

The Summer Day

Who made the world?
Who made the swan and the black bear?
Who made the grasshopper?
This grasshopper, I mean –
the one who has flung herself out of the grass,
the one who is eating sugar out of my hand,
who is moving her jaws back and forth
      instead of up and down –
who is gazing around with her enormous and
      complicated eyes.
Now she lifts her pale forearms
      and thoroughly washes her face.
Now she snaps her wings open, and floats away.
I don't know exactly what a prayer is.
I do know how to pay attention, how to fall down
into the grass, how to kneel down in the grass,
how to be idle and blessed, how to stroll through the fields,
which is what I have been doing all day.
Tell me, what else should I have done?
Doesn't everything die at last, and too soon?
Tell me, what is it you plan to do
with your one wild and precious life?

From *House of Light* by Mary Oliver
© 1990 Mary Oliver
Reprinted by permission of Beacon Press, Boston

References

Abbott, Margery Post (1997) *A certain kind of perfection: an anthology of Evangelical and Liberal Quaker writers.* Pendle Hill Publications: Wallingford, PA.

Ambler, Rex (1997) 'Experiment with Light'. Handout to workshop participants

Bacon, Margaret Hope (1980) *Valiant Friend, the life of Lucretia Mott.* Walker: New York

Baldwin, Christina (1990) *Life's companion: journal writing as a spiritual quest.* Bantam Books: New York

Berry, Thomas (1990) 'The spirituality of the earth'. In Charles Birch *et al.* (eds.) *Liberating life: contemporary approaches to ecological theology.* Orbis Books: Maryknoll, NY.

Betcher, Sharon V. (1993) 'A theology of wetness', *EarthLight*, 12, Winter 1993-4

Bownas, Samuel (1795) *An Account of the life, travels and Christian experiences in the work of the ministry of Samuel Bownas.* James Phillips: London

Bragdon, Emma (1990) *The call of spiritual emergency: from personal crisis to personal transformation.* Harper & Row: San Francisco

Braybrooke, Marcus (1990) *Time to meet: towards a deeper relationship between Jews and Christians.* SCM: London

Buber, Martin (1966) *The way of man according to the teaching of Hasidism.* Citadel Press: Seacaucus, New Jersey

Burch, Mark A. (1995) *Simplicity: notes, stories and exercises for developing unimaginable wealth.* New Society Publishers: Philadelphia, PA.

Caldwell, Christine (1996) *Getting our bodies back: recovery, healing, and transformation through body-centred psychotherapy.* Shambhala: Boston

Campbell, Joseph (1989) *This business of the gods ...* Windrose Films Ltd: Ontario

Carnes, Robin Deen and Craig, Sally (1998) *Sacred circles: a guide to creating your own women's spirituality group.* HarperSanFrancisco

Corbett, Jim (1991) *Goatwalking.* Viking/Penguin: New York

Cotter, Jim (1993) *Giving voice to the voiceless: encouraging one another in the shaping of prayer.* Selly Oak Colleges Occasional Paper No. 12: Birmingham

Crisp, Stephen (1675) 'Stephen Crisp his testimony concerning James Parnel'. In {Parnell, James}, *Collection of the Several Writings given forth from the Spirit of the Lord through that Meek, Patient and Suffering Servant of God, James Parnel.* [Colchester]

de Waal, Esther (1992) *A seven day journey with Thomas Merton.* Eagle: Guildford, Surrey

Dillard, Annie (1995) extract from *Pilgrim at Tinker Creek.* In *The Annie Dillard Reader.* Harper Perennial: New York

Edwards, Jeni (1992) *The New Age and the Church.* Bumblebee Booklets: Youlgrave, Derbyshire

Farrow, Jo (1990) *The world in my heart.* QHS: London

Fox, George (1698) *A Collection of the Many Select and Christian Epistles, Letters and Testimonies ... of ... George Fox,* Vol 2. T. Sowle: London

Fox, Matthew (1988) *The coming of the Cosmic Christ: the healing of Mother Earth and the birth of a global renaissance.* Harper & Row: Berkeley, CA.

Fox, Matthew (1991) 'Creation spirituality and the dreamtime'. In Catherine Hammond (ed.) *Creation spirituality and the dreamtime.* Millennium Books: Newtown, NSW.

Fox, Matthew (1996) *Confessions: the making of a post-denominational priest.* HarperSanFrancisco

Gorman, George (1979) *The amazing fact of Quaker worship.* QHS: London

Griffin, Susan (1995) *The eros of everyday life: essays on ecology, gender and society.* Anchor Books: New York

Gwyn, Douglas (1996) 'Sense and sensibilities: Quaker bispirituality today'. In Chuck Fager (ed.) *The Bible, the Church and the future of Friends.* The Issues Program, Pendle Hill: Wallingford, PA.

Gwyn, Douglas (1997) 'Seekers then and now', *The Seeker,* Autumn

Handy, Charles (1997) *The hungry spirit.* Hutchinson: London

Heathfield, Margaret (1994) *Being together: our corporate life in the Religious Society of Friends.* QHS & Woodbrooke College: London

Heyward, Carter (1984) *Our passion for justice: images of power, sexuality, and liberation.* The Pilgrim Press: New York

Howgill, Francis (1672) 'Francis Howgil's testimony concerning Edward Burroughs'. In {Edward Burrough}, *The memorable works of a son of thunder and consolation*. [London]

Jensen, Derrick (1995) *Listening to the land: conversations about nature, culture, and eros*. Sierra Club Books: San Francisco

Johnson, Elizabeth A. (1993) *Woman, earth and Creator Spirit*. Paulist Press: New York

Julian of Norwich (1966) *Revelations of divine love*, trans. Clifton Wolters. Penguin: Harmondsworth

Kasl, Charlotte Davis (1992) *Many roads, one journey: moving beyond the twelve steps*. HarperCollins: New York

Keen, Sam (1985) *The passionate life: stages in loving*. Gateway Books: London

Keen, Sam (1997) *Hymns to an unknown God: awakening the Spirit in everyday life*. Piatkus: London

Ketterer, Rose (1987) 'G-d/ess' Web', *Friendly Woman*, 8(1):10-11

Kovel, Joel (1983) *Against the state of nuclear terror*. Pan Books/Channel Four: London

Linn, Matthew, Linn, Sheila, and Linn, Dennis (1995) *Healing religious addiction: reclaiming healthy spirituality*. Darton, Longman & Todd: London

Loring, Patricia (1997) *Listening spirituality*, vol. 1. Openings Press: Washington, D.C.

MacMurray, John (1965) *Search for reality in religion*. George Allen and Unwin: London

Macy, Joanna (1991) *World as lover, world as self*. Parallax Press: Berkeley, CA.

Massey, Marshall (1989) *Seeking the Kingdom*. Sunderland P. Gardner Lecture, Canadian Quaker Pamphlet #33

Mykoff, Moshe (1994) *The empty chair, finding hope and joy: Rebbe Nachman of Breslov*. Jewish Lights Publishing: Woodstock, Vermont

Oliver, Mary (1986) *Dream work*. The Atlantic Monthly Press: New York

Oliver, Mary (1990) *House of light*. Beacon Press: Boston

O'Shea, Ursula (Janey) (1993) *Living the way: Quaker spirituality and community*. Australia Yearly Meeting

Parker-Rhodes, Damaris (1977) *Truth: a path and not a possession. A Quaker woman's journey*. Friends Home Service Committee: London

Peck, M. Scott (1978) *The road less travelled*. Touchstone/Simon & Schuster: New York

Penington, Isaac (1994) 'To Friends in Amersham, Aylesbury, 4th of Third Month 1667'. In *The works of Isaac Penington, a minister of the Gospel in the Society of Friends*, vol. 2. Quaker Heritage Press: Glenside, PA.

Penn, William (1765) preface to George Fox, *Journal*, third edition. Richardson & Clark: London

Penn, William (1782) *The select works of William Penn in five volumes*, 3rd edition. James Phillips: London

Penn, William (1993) *The peace of Europe, Some fruits of solitude, and other writings*, edited by Edwin B. Bonner. Everyman: London

Polkinghorne, John (1998) *Science and theology: an introduction*. SPCK/Fortress Press: London

Quaker faith and practice: the book of Christian discipline of the Yearly Meeting of the Religious Society of Friends (Quakers) in Britain (1995) BYM: London

Richards, M.C. (1990) 'Deep Ecology', *Creation*, 6(5) Sept/Oct:25

Rolston, Holmes (1996) 'Scientific Inquiry'. In Peter H. Van Ness (ed.) *Spirituality and the secular quest*. SCM: London

Seed, John *et al.* (1988) *Thinking like a mountain*. New Society Publishers: Philadelphia, PA.

Spong, John Selby (1998) *Why Christianity must change or die: a bishop speaks to believers in exile*. HarperSanFrancisco

Vining, Elizabeth Gray (1959) *Friend of life: the biography of Rufus M. Jones*. Michael Joseph: London

Walker, Alice (1989) *The temple of my familiar*. Simon & Schuster: New York

Waskow, Arthur (1978) *Godwrestling*. Schocken Books: New York

Williamson, Marianne (1992) *A return to love: reflections on the principles of A Course in Miracles*. Thorsons: London